C-3714   CAREER EXAMINATION SERIES

This is your
PASSBOOK for...

Environmental Health Specialist

Test Preparation Study Guide
Questions & Answers

NATIONAL LEARNING CORPORATION®

COPYRIGHT NOTICE

This book is SOLELY intended for, is sold ONLY to, and its use is RESTRICTED to individual, bona fide applicants or candidates who qualify by virtue of having seriously filed applications for appropriate license, certificate, professional and/or promotional advancement, higher school matriculation, scholarship, or other legitimate requirements of education and/or governmental authorities.

This book is NOT intended for use, class instruction, tutoring, training, duplication, copying, reprinting, excerption, or adaptation, etc., by:

1) Other publishers
2) Proprietors and/or Instructors of "Coaching" and/or Preparatory Courses
3) Personnel and/or Training Divisions of commercial, industrial, and governmental organizations
4) Schools, colleges, or universities and/or their departments and staffs, including teachers and other personnel
5) Testing Agencies or Bureaus
6) Study groups which seek by the purchase of a single volume to copy and/or duplicate and/or adapt this material for use by the group as a whole without having purchased individual volumes for each of the members of the group
7) Et al.

Such persons would be in violation of appropriate Federal and State statutes.

PROVISION OF LICENSING AGREEMENTS – Recognized educational, commercial, industrial, and governmental institutions and organizations, and others legitimately engaged in educational pursuits, including training, testing, and measurement activities, may address request for a licensing agreement to the copyright owners, who will determine whether, and under what conditions, including fees and charges, the materials in this book may be used them. In other words, a licensing facility exists for the legitimate use of the material in this book on other than an individual basis. However, it is asseverated and affirmed here that the material in this book CANNOT be used without the receipt of the express permission of such a licensing agreement from the Publishers. Inquiries re licensing should be addressed to the company, attention rights and permissions department.

All rights reserved, including the right of reproduction in whole or in part, in any form or by any means, electronic or mechanical, including photocopying, recording, or by any information storage and retrieval system, without permission in writing from the Publisher.

Copyright © 2024 by
National Learning Corporation

212 Michael Drive, Syosset, NY 11791
(516) 921-8888 • www.passbooks.com
E-mail: info@passbooks.com

PASSBOOK® SERIES

THE *PASSBOOK® SERIES* has been created to prepare applicants and candidates for the ultimate academic battlefield – the examination room.

At some time in our lives, each and every one of us may be required to take an examination – for validation, matriculation, admission, qualification, registration, certification, or licensure.

Based on the assumption that every applicant or candidate has met the basic formal educational standards, has taken the required number of courses, and read the necessary texts, the *PASSBOOK® SERIES* furnishes the one special preparation which may assure passing with confidence, instead of failing with insecurity. Examination questions – together with answers – are furnished as the basic vehicle for study so that the mysteries of the examination and its compounding difficulties may be eliminated or diminished by a sure method.

This book is meant to help you pass your examination provided that you qualify and are serious in your objective.

The entire field is reviewed through the huge store of content information which is succinctly presented through a provocative and challenging approach – the question-and-answer method.

A climate of success is established by furnishing the correct answers at the end of each test.

You soon learn to recognize types of questions, forms of questions, and patterns of questioning. You may even begin to anticipate expected outcomes.

You perceive that many questions are repeated or adapted so that you can gain acute insights, which may enable you to score many sure points.

You learn how to confront new questions, or types of questions, and to attack them confidently and work out the correct answers.

You note objectives and emphases, and recognize pitfalls and dangers, so that you may make positive educational adjustments.

Moreover, you are kept fully informed in relation to new concepts, methods, practices, and directions in the field.

You discover that you are actually taking the examination all the time: you are preparing for the examination by "taking" an examination, not by reading extraneous and/or supererogatory textbooks.

In short, this PASSBOOK®, used directedly, should be an important factor in helping you to pass your test.

ENVIRONMENTAL HEALTH SPECIALIST

DUTIES

Environmental health specialists inspect facilities and monitor food, air and water for unsanitary or dangerous conditions and make recommendations to alleviate such conditions. You would assist in activities to help reduce exposure to toxic substances in the environment. Typical activities may include e collecting and assembling data on exposure to toxic substances; conducting evaluations of contaminated sites; evaluating training programs and other educational efforts; reviewing inspection reports; identifying interventions to limit exposures at contaminated sites; ensuring evaluations, inspections, and interventions are carried out in accordance with statue, regulations, and approved procedures. You would also assist in reviewing scientific literature on the environmental fate of pollutants, communicating technical information to the public in a variety of settings, and determining appropriate sampling and laboratory analyses for evaluation of environmental contamination.

SUBJECT OF EXAMINATION

The written test will be designed to test for knowledge, skills, and/or abilities in such areas as:
1. Food, air and water sampling;
2. Vector and pest control;
3. Occupational and environmental safety and health;
4. Hazardous waste and materials management;
5. Inspection of housing, institutional and recreational facilities;
6. Collection, analysis, and interpretation of environmental data; and
7. Preparing written material.

HOW TO TAKE A TEST

I. YOU MUST PASS AN EXAMINATION

A. *WHAT EVERY CANDIDATE SHOULD KNOW*

Examination applicants often ask us for help in preparing for the written test. What can I study in advance? What kinds of questions will be asked? How will the test be given? How will the papers be graded?

As an applicant for a civil service examination, you may be wondering about some of these things. Our purpose here is to suggest effective methods of advance study and to describe civil service examinations.

Your chances for success on this examination can be increased if you know how to prepare. Those "pre-examination jitters" can be reduced if you know what to expect. You can even experience an adventure in good citizenship if you know why civil service exams are given.

B. *WHY ARE CIVIL SERVICE EXAMINATIONS GIVEN?*

Civil service examinations are important to you in two ways. As a citizen, you want public jobs filled by employees who know how to do their work. As a job seeker, you want a fair chance to compete for that job on an equal footing with other candidates. The best-known means of accomplishing this two-fold goal is the competitive examination.

Exams are widely publicized throughout the nation. They may be administered for jobs in federal, state, city, municipal, town or village governments or agencies.

Any citizen may apply, with some limitations, such as the age or residence of applicants. Your experience and education may be reviewed to see whether you meet the requirements for the particular examination. When these requirements exist, they are reasonable and applied consistently to all applicants. Thus, a competitive examination may cause you some uneasiness now, but it is your privilege and safeguard.

C. *HOW ARE CIVIL SERVICE EXAMS DEVELOPED?*

Examinations are carefully written by trained technicians who are specialists in the field known as "psychological measurement," in consultation with recognized authorities in the field of work that the test will cover. These experts recommend the subject matter areas or skills to be tested; only those knowledges or skills important to your success on the job are included. The most reliable books and source materials available are used as references. Together, the experts and technicians judge the difficulty level of the questions.

Test technicians know how to phrase questions so that the problem is clearly stated. Their ethics do not permit "trick" or "catch" questions. Questions may have been tried out on sample groups, or subjected to statistical analysis, to determine their usefulness.

Written tests are often used in combination with performance tests, ratings of training and experience, and oral interviews. All of these measures combine to form the best-known means of finding the right person for the right job.

II. HOW TO PASS THE WRITTEN TEST

A. NATURE OF THE EXAMINATION

To prepare intelligently for civil service examinations, you should know how they differ from school examinations you have taken. In school you were assigned certain definite pages to read or subjects to cover. The examination questions were quite detailed and usually emphasized memory. Civil service exams, on the other hand, try to discover your present ability to perform the duties of a position, plus your potentiality to learn these duties. In other words, a civil service exam attempts to predict how successful you will be. Questions cover such a broad area that they cannot be as minute and detailed as school exam questions.

In the public service similar kinds of work, or positions, are grouped together in one "class." This process is known as *position-classification*. All the positions in a class are paid according to the salary range for that class. One class title covers all of these positions, and they are all tested by the same examination.

B. FOUR BASIC STEPS

1) Study the announcement

How, then, can you know what subjects to study? Our best answer is: "Learn as much as possible about the class of positions for which you've applied." The exam will test the knowledge, skills and abilities needed to do the work.

Your most valuable source of information about the position you want is the official exam announcement. This announcement lists the training and experience qualifications. Check these standards and apply only if you come reasonably close to meeting them.

The brief description of the position in the examination announcement offers some clues to the subjects which will be tested. Think about the job itself. Review the duties in your mind. Can you perform them, or are there some in which you are rusty? Fill in the blank spots in your preparation.

Many jurisdictions preview the written test in the exam announcement by including a section called "Knowledge and Abilities Required," "Scope of the Examination," or some similar heading. Here you will find out specifically what fields will be tested.

2) Review your own background

Once you learn in general what the position is all about, and what you need to know to do the work, ask yourself which subjects you already know fairly well and which need improvement. You may wonder whether to concentrate on improving your strong areas or on building some background in your fields of weakness. When the announcement has specified "some knowledge" or "considerable knowledge," or has used adjectives like "beginning principles of…" or "advanced … methods," you can get a clue as to the number and difficulty of questions to be asked in any given field. More questions, and hence broader coverage, would be included for those subjects which are more important in the work. Now weigh your strengths and weaknesses against the job requirements and prepare accordingly.

3) Determine the level of the position

Another way to tell how intensively you should prepare is to understand the level of the job for which you are applying. Is it the entering level? In other words, is this the position in which beginners in a field of work are hired? Or is it an intermediate or advanced level? Sometimes this is indicated by such words as "Junior" or "Senior" in the class title. Other jurisdictions use Roman numerals to designate the level – Clerk I, Clerk II, for example. The word "Supervisor" sometimes appears in the title. If the level is not indicated by the title, check the description of duties. Will you be working under very close supervision, or will you have responsibility for independent decisions in this work?

4) Choose appropriate study materials

Now that you know the subjects to be examined and the relative amount of each subject to be covered, you can choose suitable study materials. For beginning level jobs, or even advanced ones, if you have a pronounced weakness in some aspect of your training, read a modern, standard textbook in that field. Be sure it is up to date and has general coverage. Such books are normally available at your library, and the librarian will be glad to help you locate one. For entry-level positions, questions of appropriate difficulty are chosen – neither highly advanced questions, nor those too simple. Such questions require careful thought but not advanced training.

If the position for which you are applying is technical or advanced, you will read more advanced, specialized material. If you are already familiar with the basic principles of your field, elementary textbooks would waste your time. Concentrate on advanced textbooks and technical periodicals. Think through the concepts and review difficult problems in your field.

These are all general sources. You can get more ideas on your own initiative, following these leads. For example, training manuals and publications of the government agency which employs workers in your field can be useful, particularly for technical and professional positions. A letter or visit to the government department involved may result in more specific study suggestions, and certainly will provide you with a more definite idea of the exact nature of the position you are seeking.

III. KINDS OF TESTS

Tests are used for purposes other than measuring knowledge and ability to perform specified duties. For some positions, it is equally important to test ability to make adjustments to new situations or to profit from training. In others, basic mental abilities not dependent on information are essential. Questions which test these things may not appear as pertinent to the duties of the position as those which test for knowledge and information. Yet they are often highly important parts of a fair examination. For very general questions, it is almost impossible to help you direct your study efforts. What we can do is to point out some of the more common of these general abilities needed in public service positions and describe some typical questions.

1) General information

Broad, general information has been found useful for predicting job success in some kinds of work. This is tested in a variety of ways, from vocabulary lists to questions about current events. Basic background in some field of work, such as sociology or economics, may be sampled in a group of questions. Often these are principles which have become familiar to most persons through exposure rather than through formal training. It is difficult to advise you how to study for these questions; being alert to the world around you is our best suggestion.

2) Verbal ability

An example of an ability needed in many positions is verbal or language ability. Verbal ability is, in brief, the ability to use and understand words. Vocabulary and grammar tests are typical measures of this ability. Reading comprehension or paragraph interpretation questions are common in many kinds of civil service tests. You are given a paragraph of written material and asked to find its central meaning.

3) Numerical ability

Number skills can be tested by the familiar arithmetic problem, by checking paired lists of numbers to see which are alike and which are different, or by interpreting charts and graphs. In the latter test, a graph may be printed in the test booklet which you are asked to use as the basis for answering questions.

4) Observation

A popular test for law-enforcement positions is the observation test. A picture is shown to you for several minutes, then taken away. Questions about the picture test your ability to observe both details and larger elements.

5) Following directions

In many positions in the public service, the employee must be able to carry out written instructions dependably and accurately. You may be given a chart with several columns, each column listing a variety of information. The questions require you to carry out directions involving the information given in the chart.

6) Skills and aptitudes

Performance tests effectively measure some manual skills and aptitudes. When the skill is one in which you are trained, such as typing or shorthand, you can practice. These tests are often very much like those given in business school or high school courses. For many of the other skills and aptitudes, however, no short-time preparation can be made. Skills and abilities natural to you or that you have developed throughout your lifetime are being tested.

Many of the general questions just described provide all the data needed to answer the questions and ask you to use your reasoning ability to find the answers. Your best preparation for these tests, as well as for tests of facts and ideas, is to be at your physical and mental best. You, no doubt, have your own methods of getting into an exam-taking mood and keeping "in shape." The next section lists some ideas on this subject.

IV. KINDS OF QUESTIONS

Only rarely is the "essay" question, which you answer in narrative form, used in civil service tests. Civil service tests are usually of the short-answer type. Full instructions for answering these questions will be given to you at the examination. But in case this is your first experience with short-answer questions and separate answer sheets, here is what you need to know:

1) Multiple-choice Questions

Most popular of the short-answer questions is the "multiple choice" or "best answer" question. It can be used, for example, to test for factual knowledge, ability to solve problems or judgment in meeting situations found at work.

A multiple-choice question is normally one of three types—
- It can begin with an incomplete statement followed by several possible endings. You are to find the one ending which *best* completes the statement, although some of the others may not be entirely wrong.
- It can also be a complete statement in the form of a question which is answered by choosing one of the statements listed.

- It can be in the form of a problem – again you select the best answer.

Here is an example of a multiple-choice question with a discussion which should give you some clues as to the method for choosing the right answer:

When an employee has a complaint about his assignment, the action which will *best* help him overcome his difficulty is to
  A. discuss his difficulty with his coworkers
  B. take the problem to the head of the organization
  C. take the problem to the person who gave him the assignment
  D. say nothing to anyone about his complaint

In answering this question, you should study each of the choices to find which is best. Consider choice "A" – Certainly an employee may discuss his complaint with fellow employees, but no change or improvement can result, and the complaint remains unresolved. Choice "B" is a poor choice since the head of the organization probably does not know what assignment you have been given, and taking your problem to him is known as "going over the head" of the supervisor. The supervisor, or person who made the assignment, is the person who can clarify it or correct any injustice. Choice "C" is, therefore, correct. To say nothing, as in choice "D," is unwise. Supervisors have and interest in knowing the problems employees are facing, and the employee is seeking a solution to his problem.

2) True/False Questions

The "true/false" or "right/wrong" form of question is sometimes used. Here a complete statement is given. Your job is to decide whether the statement is right or wrong.

SAMPLE: A roaming cell-phone call to a nearby city costs less than a non-roaming call to a distant city.

This statement is wrong, or false, since roaming calls are more expensive.

This is not a complete list of all possible question forms, although most of the others are variations of these common types. You will always get complete directions for answering questions. Be sure you understand *how* to mark your answers – ask questions until you do.

V. RECORDING YOUR ANSWERS

Computer terminals are used more and more today for many different kinds of exams.
For an examination with very few applicants, you may be told to record your answers in the test booklet itself. Separate answer sheets are much more common. If this separate answer sheet is to be scored by machine – and this is often the case – it is highly important that you mark your answers correctly in order to get credit.

An electronic scoring machine is often used in civil service offices because of the speed with which papers can be scored. Machine-scored answer sheets must be marked with a pencil, which will be given to you. This pencil has a high graphite content which responds to the electronic scoring machine. As a matter of fact, stray dots may register as answers, so do not let your pencil rest on the answer sheet while you are pondering the correct answer. Also, if your pencil lead breaks or is otherwise defective, ask for another.

Since the answer sheet will be dropped in a slot in the scoring machine, be careful not to bend the corners or get the paper crumpled.

The answer sheet normally has five vertical columns of numbers, with 30 numbers to a column. These numbers correspond to the question numbers in your test booklet. After each number, going across the page are four or five pairs of dotted lines. These short dotted lines have small letters or numbers above them. The first two pairs may also have a "T" or "F" above the letters. This indicates that the first two pairs only are to be used if the questions are of the true-false type. If the questions are multiple choice, disregard the "T" and "F" and pay attention only to the small letters or numbers.

Answer your questions in the manner of the sample that follows:

32. The largest city in the United States is
    A. Washington, D.C.
    B. New York City
    C. Chicago
    D. Detroit
    E. San Francisco

1) Choose the answer you think is best. (New York City is the largest, so "B" is correct.)
2) Find the row of dotted lines numbered the same as the question you are answering. (Find row number 32)
3) Find the pair of dotted lines corresponding to the answer. (Find the pair of lines under the mark "B.")
4) Make a solid black mark between the dotted lines.

VI. BEFORE THE TEST

Common sense will help you find procedures to follow to get ready for an examination. Too many of us, however, overlook these sensible measures. Indeed, nervousness and fatigue have been found to be the most serious reasons why applicants fail to do their best on civil service tests. Here is a list of reminders:

- Begin your preparation early – Don't wait until the last minute to go scurrying around for books and materials or to find out what the position is all about.
- Prepare continuously – An hour a night for a week is better than an all-night cram session. This has been definitely established. What is more, a night a week for a month will return better dividends than crowding your study into a shorter period of time.
- Locate the place of the exam – You have been sent a notice telling you when and where to report for the examination. If the location is in a different town or otherwise unfamiliar to you, it would be well to inquire the best route and learn something about the building.
- Relax the night before the test – Allow your mind to rest. Do not study at all that night. Plan some mild recreation or diversion; then go to bed early and get a good night's sleep.
- Get up early enough to make a leisurely trip to the place for the test – This way unforeseen events, traffic snarls, unfamiliar buildings, etc. will not upset you.
- Dress comfortably – A written test is not a fashion show. You will be known by number and not by name, so wear something comfortable.

- Leave excess paraphernalia at home – Shopping bags and odd bundles will get in your way. You need bring only the items mentioned in the official notice you received; usually everything you need is provided. Do not bring reference books to the exam. They will only confuse those last minutes and be taken away from you when in the test room.
- Arrive somewhat ahead of time – If because of transportation schedules you must get there very early, bring a newspaper or magazine to take your mind off yourself while waiting.
- Locate the examination room – When you have found the proper room, you will be directed to the seat or part of the room where you will sit. Sometimes you are given a sheet of instructions to read while you are waiting. Do not fill out any forms until you are told to do so; just read them and be prepared.
- Relax and prepare to listen to the instructions
- If you have any physical problem that may keep you from doing your best, be sure to tell the test administrator. If you are sick or in poor health, you really cannot do your best on the exam. You can come back and take the test some other time.

VII. AT THE TEST

The day of the test is here and you have the test booklet in your hand. The temptation to get going is very strong. Caution! There is more to success than knowing the right answers. You must know how to identify your papers and understand variations in the type of short-answer question used in this particular examination. Follow these suggestions for maximum results from your efforts:

1) Cooperate with the monitor

The test administrator has a duty to create a situation in which you can be as much at ease as possible. He will give instructions, tell you when to begin, check to see that you are marking your answer sheet correctly, and so on. He is not there to guard you, although he will see that your competitors do not take unfair advantage. He wants to help you do your best.

2) Listen to all instructions

Don't jump the gun! Wait until you understand all directions. In most civil service tests you get more time than you need to answer the questions. So don't be in a hurry. Read each word of instructions until you clearly understand the meaning. Study the examples, listen to all announcements and follow directions. Ask questions if you do not understand what to do.

3) Identify your papers

Civil service exams are usually identified by number only. You will be assigned a number; you must not put your name on your test papers. Be sure to copy your number correctly. Since more than one exam may be given, copy your exact examination title.

4) Plan your time

Unless you are told that a test is a "speed" or "rate of work" test, speed itself is usually not important. Time enough to answer all the questions will be provided, but this does not mean that you have all day. An overall time limit has been set. Divide the total time (in minutes) by the number of questions to determine the approximate time you have for each question.

5) Do not linger over difficult questions

If you come across a difficult question, mark it with a paper clip (useful to have along) and come back to it when you have been through the booklet. One caution if you do this – be sure to skip a number on your answer sheet as well. Check often to be sure that you have not lost your place and that you are marking in the row numbered the same as the question you are answering.

6) Read the questions

Be sure you know what the question asks! Many capable people are unsuccessful because they failed to *read* the questions correctly.

7) Answer all questions

Unless you have been instructed that a penalty will be deducted for incorrect answers, it is better to guess than to omit a question.

8) Speed tests

It is often better NOT to guess on speed tests. It has been found that on timed tests people are tempted to spend the last few seconds before time is called in marking answers at random – without even reading them – in the hope of picking up a few extra points. To discourage this practice, the instructions may warn you that your score will be "corrected" for guessing. That is, a penalty will be applied. The incorrect answers will be deducted from the correct ones, or some other penalty formula will be used.

9) Review your answers

If you finish before time is called, go back to the questions you guessed or omitted to give them further thought. Review other answers if you have time.

10) Return your test materials

If you are ready to leave before others have finished or time is called, take ALL your materials to the monitor and leave quietly. Never take any test material with you. The monitor can discover whose papers are not complete, and taking a test booklet may be grounds for disqualification.

VIII. EXAMINATION TECHNIQUES

1) Read the general instructions carefully. These are usually printed on the first page of the exam booklet. As a rule, these instructions refer to the timing of the examination; the fact that you should not start work until the signal and must stop work at a signal, etc. If there are any *special* instructions, such as a choice of questions to be answered, make sure that you note this instruction carefully.

2) When you are ready to start work on the examination, that is as soon as the signal has been given, read the instructions to each question booklet, underline any key words or phrases, such as *least, best, outline, describe* and the like. In this way you will tend to answer as requested rather than discover on reviewing your paper that you *listed without describing*, that you selected the *worst* choice rather than the *best* choice, etc.

3) If the examination is of the objective or multiple-choice type – that is, each question will also give a series of possible answers: A, B, C or D, and you are called upon to select the best answer and write the letter next to that answer on your answer paper – it is advisable to start answering each question in turn. There may be anywhere from 50 to 100 such questions in the three or four hours allotted and you can see how much time would be taken if you read through all the questions before beginning to answer any. Furthermore, if you come across a question or group of questions which you know would be difficult to answer, it would undoubtedly affect your handling of all the other questions.

4) If the examination is of the essay type and contains but a few questions, it is a moot point as to whether you should read all the questions before starting to answer any one. Of course, if you are given a choice – say five out of seven and the like – then it is essential to read all the questions so you can eliminate the two that are most difficult. If, however, you are asked to answer all the questions, there may be danger in trying to answer the easiest one first because you may find that you will spend too much time on it. The best technique is to answer the first question, then proceed to the second, etc.

5) Time your answers. Before the exam begins, write down the time it started, then add the time allowed for the examination and write down the time it must be completed, then divide the time available somewhat as follows:
    - If 3-1/2 hours are allowed, that would be 210 minutes. If you have 80 objective-type questions, that would be an average of 2-1/2 minutes per question. Allow yourself no more than 2 minutes per question, or a total of 160 minutes, which will permit about 50 minutes to review.
    - If for the time allotment of 210 minutes there are 7 essay questions to answer, that would average about 30 minutes a question. Give yourself only 25 minutes per question so that you have about 35 minutes to review.

6) The most important instruction is to *read each question* and make sure you know what is wanted. The second most important instruction is to *time yourself properly* so that you answer every question. The third most important instruction is to *answer every question*. Guess if you have to but include something for each question. Remember that you will receive no credit for a blank and will probably receive some credit if you write something in answer to an essay question. If you guess a letter – say "B" for a multiple-choice question – you may have guessed right. If you leave a blank as an answer to a multiple-choice question, the examiners may respect your feelings but it will not add a point to your score. Some exams may penalize you for wrong answers, so in such cases *only*, you may not want to guess unless you have some basis for your answer.

7) Suggestions
    a. Objective-type questions
        1. Examine the question booklet for proper sequence of pages and questions
        2. Read all instructions carefully
        3. Skip any question which seems too difficult; return to it after all other questions have been answered
        4. Apportion your time properly; do not spend too much time on any single question or group of questions

5. Note and underline key words – *all, most, fewest, least, best, worst, same, opposite,* etc.
6. Pay particular attention to negatives
7. Note unusual option, e.g., unduly long, short, complex, different or similar in content to the body of the question
8. Observe the use of "hedging" words – *probably, may, most likely,* etc.
9. Make sure that your answer is put next to the same number as the question
10. Do not second-guess unless you have good reason to believe the second answer is definitely more correct
11. Cross out original answer if you decide another answer is more accurate; do not erase until you are ready to hand your paper in
12. Answer all questions; guess unless instructed otherwise
13. Leave time for review

b. Essay questions
1. Read each question carefully
2. Determine exactly what is wanted. Underline key words or phrases.
3. Decide on outline or paragraph answer
4. Include many different points and elements unless asked to develop any one or two points or elements
5. Show impartiality by giving pros and cons unless directed to select one side only
6. Make and write down any assumptions you find necessary to answer the questions
7. Watch your English, grammar, punctuation and choice of words
8. Time your answers; don't crowd material

8) Answering the essay question

Most essay questions can be answered by framing the specific response around several key words or ideas. Here are a few such key words or ideas:

M's: manpower, materials, methods, money, management
P's: purpose, program, policy, plan, procedure, practice, problems, pitfalls, personnel, public relations

a. Six basic steps in handling problems:
1. Preliminary plan and background development
2. Collect information, data and facts
3. Analyze and interpret information, data and facts
4. Analyze and develop solutions as well as make recommendations
5. Prepare report and sell recommendations
6. Install recommendations and follow up effectiveness

b. Pitfalls to avoid
1. *Taking things for granted* – A statement of the situation does not necessarily imply that each of the elements is necessarily true; for example, a complaint may be invalid and biased so that all that can be taken for granted is that a complaint has been registered

2. *Considering only one side of a situation* – Wherever possible, indicate several alternatives and then point out the reasons you selected the best one
3. *Failing to indicate follow up* – Whenever your answer indicates action on your part, make certain that you will take proper follow-up action to see how successful your recommendations, procedures or actions turn out to be
4. *Taking too long in answering any single question* – Remember to time your answers properly

IX. AFTER THE TEST

Scoring procedures differ in detail among civil service jurisdictions although the general principles are the same. Whether the papers are hand-scored or graded by machine we have described, they are nearly always graded by number. That is, the person who marks the paper knows only the number – never the name – of the applicant. Not until all the papers have been graded will they be matched with names. If other tests, such as training and experience or oral interview ratings have been given, scores will be combined. Different parts of the examination usually have different weights. For example, the written test might count 60 percent of the final grade, and a rating of training and experience 40 percent. In many jurisdictions, veterans will have a certain number of points added to their grades.

After the final grade has been determined, the names are placed in grade order and an eligible list is established. There are various methods for resolving ties between those who get the same final grade – probably the most common is to place first the name of the person whose application was received first. Job offers are made from the eligible list in the order the names appear on it. You will be notified of your grade and your rank as soon as all these computations have been made. This will be done as rapidly as possible.

People who are found to meet the requirements in the announcement are called "eligibles." Their names are put on a list of eligible candidates. An eligible's chances of getting a job depend on how high he stands on this list and how fast agencies are filling jobs from the list.

When a job is to be filled from a list of eligibles, the agency asks for the names of people on the list of eligibles for that job. When the civil service commission receives this request, it sends to the agency the names of the three people highest on this list. Or, if the job to be filled has specialized requirements, the office sends the agency the names of the top three persons who meet these requirements from the general list.

The appointing officer makes a choice from among the three people whose names were sent to him. If the selected person accepts the appointment, the names of the others are put back on the list to be considered for future openings.

That is the rule in hiring from all kinds of eligible lists, whether they are for typist, carpenter, chemist, or something else. For every vacancy, the appointing officer has his choice of any one of the top three eligibles on the list. This explains why the person whose name is on top of the list sometimes does not get an appointment when some of the persons lower on the list do. If the appointing officer chooses the second or third eligible, the No. 1 eligible does not get a job at once, but stays on the list until he is appointed or the list is terminated.

X. HOW TO PASS THE INTERVIEW TEST

The examination for which you applied requires an oral interview test. You have already taken the written test and you are now being called for the interview test – the final part of the formal examination.

You may think that it is not possible to prepare for an interview test and that there are no procedures to follow during an interview. Our purpose is to point out some things you can do in advance that will help you and some good rules to follow and pitfalls to avoid while you are being interviewed.

What is an interview supposed to test?

The written examination is designed to test the technical knowledge and competence of the candidate; the oral is designed to evaluate intangible qualities, not readily measured otherwise, and to establish a list showing the relative fitness of each candidate – as measured against his competitors – for the position sought. Scoring is not on the basis of "right" and "wrong," but on a sliding scale of values ranging from "not passable" to "outstanding." As a matter of fact, it is possible to achieve a relatively low score without a single "incorrect" answer because of evident weakness in the qualities being measured.

Occasionally, an examination may consist entirely of an oral test – either an individual or a group oral. In such cases, information is sought concerning the technical knowledges and abilities of the candidate, since there has been no written examination for this purpose. More commonly, however, an oral test is used to supplement a written examination.

Who conducts interviews?

The composition of oral boards varies among different jurisdictions. In nearly all, a representative of the personnel department serves as chairman. One of the members of the board may be a representative of the department in which the candidate would work. In some cases, "outside experts" are used, and, frequently, a businessman or some other representative of the general public is asked to serve. Labor and management or other special groups may be represented. The aim is to secure the services of experts in the appropriate field.

However the board is composed, it is a good idea (and not at all improper or unethical) to ascertain in advance of the interview who the members are and what groups they represent. When you are introduced to them, you will have some idea of their backgrounds and interests, and at least you will not stutter and stammer over their names.

What should be done before the interview?

While knowledge about the board members is useful and takes some of the surprise element out of the interview, there is other preparation which is more substantive. It *is* possible to prepare for an oral interview – in several ways:

1) Keep a copy of your application and review it carefully before the interview

This may be the only document before the oral board, and the starting point of the interview. Know what education and experience you have listed there, and the sequence and dates of all of it. Sometimes the board will ask you to review the highlights of your experience for them; you should not have to hem and haw doing it.

2) Study the class specification and the examination announcement

Usually, the oral board has one or both of these to guide them. The qualities, characteristics or knowledges required by the position sought are stated in these documents. They offer valuable clues as to the nature of the oral interview. For example, if the job involves supervisory responsibilities, the announcement will usually indicate that knowledge of modern supervisory methods and the qualifications of the candidate as a supervisor will be tested. If so, you can expect such questions, frequently in the form of a hypothetical situation which you are expected to solve. NEVER go into an oral without knowledge of the duties and responsibilities of the job you seek.

3) Think through each qualification required

Try to visualize the kind of questions you would ask if you were a board member. How well could you answer them? Try especially to appraise your own knowledge and background in each area, *measured against the job sought*, and identify any areas in which you are weak. Be critical and realistic – do not flatter yourself.

4) Do some general reading in areas in which you feel you may be weak

For example, if the job involves supervision and your past experience has NOT, some general reading in supervisory methods and practices, particularly in the field of human relations, might be useful. Do NOT study agency procedures or detailed manuals. The oral board will be testing your understanding and capacity, not your memory.

5) Get a good night's sleep and watch your general health and mental attitude

You will want a clear head at the interview. Take care of a cold or any other minor ailment, and of course, no hangovers.

What should be done on the day of the interview?

Now comes the day of the interview itself. Give yourself plenty of time to get there. Plan to arrive somewhat ahead of the scheduled time, particularly if your appointment is in the fore part of the day. If a previous candidate fails to appear, the board might be ready for you a bit early. By early afternoon an oral board is almost invariably behind schedule if there are many candidates, and you may have to wait. Take along a book or magazine to read, or your application to review, but leave any extraneous material in the waiting room when you go in for your interview. In any event, relax and compose yourself.

The matter of dress is important. The board is forming impressions about you – from your experience, your manners, your attitude, and your appearance. Give your personal appearance careful attention. Dress your best, but not your flashiest. Choose conservative, appropriate clothing, and be sure it is immaculate. This is a business interview, and your appearance should indicate that you regard it as such. Besides, being well groomed and properly dressed will help boost your confidence.

Sooner or later, someone will call your name and escort you into the interview room. *This is it.* From here on you are on your own. It is too late for any more preparation. But remember, you asked for this opportunity to prove your fitness, and you are here because your request was granted.

What happens when you go in?

The usual sequence of events will be as follows: The clerk (who is often the board stenographer) will introduce you to the chairman of the oral board, who will introduce you to the other members of the board. Acknowledge the introductions before you sit down. Do not be surprised if you find a microphone facing you or a stenotypist sitting by. Oral interviews are usually recorded in the event of an appeal or other review.

Usually the chairman of the board will open the interview by reviewing the highlights of your education and work experience from your application – primarily for the benefit of the other members of the board, as well as to get the material into the record. Do not interrupt or comment unless there is an error or significant misinterpretation; if that is the case, do not hesitate. But do not quibble about insignificant matters. Also, he will usually ask you some question about your education, experience or your present job – partly to get you to start talking and to establish the interviewing "rapport." He may start the actual questioning, or turn it over to one of the other members. Frequently, each member undertakes the questioning on a particular area, one in which he is perhaps most competent, so you can expect each member to participate in the examination. Because time is limited, you may also expect some rather abrupt switches in the direction the questioning takes, so do not be upset by it. Normally, a board member will not pursue a single line of questioning unless he discovers a particular strength or weakness.

After each member has participated, the chairman will usually ask whether any member has any further questions, then will ask you if you have anything you wish to add. Unless you are expecting this question, it may floor you. Worse, it may start you off on an extended, extemporaneous speech. The board is not usually seeking more information. The question is principally to offer you a last opportunity to present further qualifications or to indicate that you have nothing to add. So, if you feel that a significant qualification or characteristic has been overlooked, it is proper to point it out in a sentence or so. Do not compliment the board on the thoroughness of their examination – they have been sketchy, and you know it. If you wish, merely say, "No thank you, I have nothing further to add." This is a point where you can "talk yourself out" of a good impression or fail to present an important bit of information. Remember, *you close the interview yourself*.

The chairman will then say, "That is all, Mr. _____, thank you." Do not be startled; the interview is over, and quicker than you think. Thank him, gather your belongings and take your leave. Save your sigh of relief for the other side of the door.

How to put your best foot forward

Throughout this entire process, you may feel that the board individually and collectively is trying to pierce your defenses, seek out your hidden weaknesses and embarrass and confuse you. Actually, this is not true. They are obliged to make an appraisal of your qualifications for the job you are seeking, and they want to see you in your best light. Remember, they must interview all candidates and a non-cooperative candidate may become a failure in spite of their best efforts to bring out his qualifications. Here are 15 suggestions that will help you:

1) Be natural – Keep your attitude confident, not cocky

If you are not confident that you can do the job, do not expect the board to be. Do not apologize for your weaknesses, try to bring out your strong points. The board is interested in a positive, not negative, presentation. Cockiness will antagonize any board member and make him wonder if you are covering up a weakness by a false show of strength.

2) Get comfortable, but don't lounge or sprawl

Sit erectly but not stiffly. A careless posture may lead the board to conclude that you are careless in other things, or at least that you are not impressed by the importance of the occasion. Either conclusion is natural, even if incorrect. Do not fuss with your clothing, a pencil or an ashtray. Your hands may occasionally be useful to emphasize a point; do not let them become a point of distraction.

3) Do not wisecrack or make small talk

This is a serious situation, and your attitude should show that you consider it as such. Further, the time of the board is limited – they do not want to waste it, and neither should you.

4) **Do not exaggerate your experience or abilities**

In the first place, from information in the application or other interviews and sources, the board may know more about you than you think. Secondly, you probably will not get away with it. An experienced board is rather adept at spotting such a situation, so do not take the chance.

5) **If you know a board member, do not make a point of it, yet do not hide it**

Certainly you are not fooling him, and probably not the other members of the board. Do not try to take advantage of your acquaintanceship – it will probably do you little good.

6) **Do not dominate the interview**

Let the board do that. They will give you the clues – do not assume that you have to do all the talking. Realize that the board has a number of questions to ask you, and do not try to take up all the interview time by showing off your extensive knowledge of the answer to the first one.

7) **Be attentive**

You only have 20 minutes or so, and you should keep your attention at its sharpest throughout. When a member is addressing a problem or question to you, give him your undivided attention. Address your reply principally to him, but do not exclude the other board members.

8) **Do not interrupt**

A board member may be stating a problem for you to analyze. He will ask you a question when the time comes. Let him state the problem, and wait for the question.

9) **Make sure you understand the question**

Do not try to answer until you are sure what the question is. If it is not clear, restate it in your own words or ask the board member to clarify it for you. However, do not haggle about minor elements.

10) **Reply promptly but not hastily**

A common entry on oral board rating sheets is "candidate responded readily," or "candidate hesitated in replies." Respond as promptly and quickly as you can, but do not jump to a hasty, ill-considered answer.

11) **Do not be peremptory in your answers**

A brief answer is proper – but do not fire your answer back. That is a losing game from your point of view. The board member can probably ask questions much faster than you can answer them.

12) **Do not try to create the answer you think the board member wants**

He is interested in what kind of mind you have and how it works – not in playing games. Furthermore, he can usually spot this practice and will actually grade you down on it.

13) **Do not switch sides in your reply merely to agree with a board member**

Frequently, a member will take a contrary position merely to draw you out and to see if you are willing and able to defend your point of view. Do not start a debate, yet do not surrender a good position. If a position is worth taking, it is worth defending.

14) Do not be afraid to admit an error in judgment if you are shown to be wrong

The board knows that you are forced to reply without any opportunity for careful consideration. Your answer may be demonstrably wrong. If so, admit it and get on with the interview.

15) Do not dwell at length on your present job

The opening question may relate to your present assignment. Answer the question but do not go into an extended discussion. You are being examined for a *new* job, not your present one. As a matter of fact, try to phrase ALL your answers in terms of the job for which you are being examined.

Basis of Rating

Probably you will forget most of these "do's" and "don'ts" when you walk into the oral interview room. Even remembering them all will not ensure you a passing grade. Perhaps you did not have the qualifications in the first place. But remembering them will help you to put your best foot forward, without treading on the toes of the board members.

Rumor and popular opinion to the contrary notwithstanding, an oral board wants you to make the best appearance possible. They know you are under pressure – but they also want to see how you respond to it as a guide to what your reaction would be under the pressures of the job you seek. They will be influenced by the degree of poise you display, the personal traits you show and the manner in which you respond.

ABOUT THIS BOOK

This book contains tests divided into Examination Sections. Go through each test, answering every question in the margin. We have also attached a sample answer sheet at the back of the book that can be removed and used. At the end of each test look at the answer key and check your answers. On the ones you got wrong, look at the right answer choice and learn. Do not fill in the answers first. Do not memorize the questions and answers, but understand the answer and principles involved. On your test, the questions will likely be different from the samples. Questions are changed and new ones added. If you understand these past questions you should have success with any changes that arise. Tests may consist of several types of questions. We have additional books on each subject should more study be advisable or necessary for you. Finally, the more you study, the better prepared you will be. This book is intended to be the last thing you study before you walk into the examination room. Prior study of relevant texts is also recommended. NLC publishes some of these in our Fundamental Series. Knowledge and good sense are important factors in passing your exam. Good luck also helps. So now study this Passbook, absorb the material contained within and take that knowledge into the examination. Then do your best to pass that exam.

EXAMINATION SECTION

EXAMINATION SECTION
TEST 1

DIRECTIONS: Each question or incomplete statement is followed by several suggested answers or completions. Select the one that BEST answers the question or completes the statement. *PRINT THE LETTER OF THE CORRECANSWER IN THE SPACE AT THE RIGHT.*

1. Which of the following biomes is characterized by trees scattered widely among dense grasses?　　1._____

    A. Prairie　　B. Savanna　　C. Veldt　　D. Steppe

2. Which of the following are most likely to be point sources of pollution?　　2._____

    A. Lawns　　　　　　　　B. Streets
    C. Industrial plants　　　D. Crop fields

3. Which of the following gases is MOST effective at trapping infrared radiation near the earth's surface?　　3._____

    A. Methane　　　　　B. Carbon dioxide
    C. Nitrous oxide　　　D. Freon CFC-11

4. Stationary air pollution sources that generate pollutants from open areas exposed to wind processes are described as _____ sources.　　4._____

    A. fugitive　　　B. nonpoint
    C. hard-path　　D. endemic

5. Which of the following is an example of secondary pollution and waste prevention?　　5._____

    A. Burying waste in landfills
    B. Reducing packaging and materials in products
    C. Using less harmful products
    D. Recycling

6. Currently, the world population is said to be increasing at a rate of about _____% annually.　　6._____

    A. 0.5　　B. 2　　C. 7　　D. 10

7. Which of the following is a reactive method for reducing the amount of air pollutants from stationary sources such as coal-burning and industrial plants?　　7._____

    A. Converting coal to a liquid or gaseous fuel
    B. Taxing each unit of pollution produced
    C. Burning low-sulfur coal
    D. Shifting to less polluting fuels

8. The simplest hydrocarbon is　　8._____

    A. propane　　B. butane　　C. methane　　D. siloxane

9. The leading nonpoint source of water pollution is

    A. leachate from solid waste disposal sites
    B. surface mine drainage
    C. industrial wastes
    D. agricultural runoff

10. Which of the following countries is most clearly a net food importer?

    A. India   B. Argentina   C. Japan   D. China

11. Which of the following are NOT harmful elements of photochemical smog?

    A. Peroxyacyl nitrates (PANs)
    B. Aldehydes
    C. Polychlorinated biphenyls (PCBs)
    D. Ozone

12. Which of the following is LEAST likely to be an environmental consequence of the recovery process in petroleum production?

    A. Land subsidence
    B. Pollution of groundwater sources
    C. Disruption of land surface
    D. Release of carbon dioxide into atmosphere

13. Which of the following terms is used to describe the upper layer of the ocean, penetrable by the sun's rays?

    A. Benthic   B. Pelagic   C. Eutrophic   D. Littoral

14. Except for designated wilderness areas, the lands of the United States Forest System are managed under the principles of

    A. preservation and resource conservation
    B. restricted use and wildlife management
    C. wise-use and industrial ecology
    D. multiple-use and sustainable yield

15. Which of the following is an example of a density-dependent factor that helps determine population fluctuations?

    A. Destruction of habitat by fire, flood, etc.
    B. Weather conditions
    C. The drying up of a small pond
    D. Food supply

16. Which of the following is NOT a typical cause of desertification?

    A. Bad farming practices
    B. Conversion of cropland to rangeland in marginal areas
    C. Overgrazing
    D. Poor forestry

17. Which of the following detritivores is a decomposer?   17.____

    A. Earthworm   B. Tree fungus
    C. Crab   D. Termite

18. Currently, which of the following is NOT a commonly used method for the disposal of   18.____
    hazardous wastes?

    A. Landfills   B. Deep-well injections
    C. Surface impoundments   D. Incineration

19. A chemical, ionizing agent, or virus that causes birth defects is termed a   19.____

    A. carcinogen   B. teratogen
    C. mutagen   D. kerogen

20. In the less developed countries of the world, pressure on agricultural resources is   20.____
    increasing. A consequence of this is that people in less developed countries

    I. are at a greater risk of protein deficiency
    II. are generally nomadic
    III. feed at lower trophic levels

    The CORRECT answer is:

    A. I, II   B. I, III   C. II, III   D. I, II, III

21. Which of the following is most commonly a source of surface water pollution, rather than   21.____
    groundwater?

    A. Saltwater intrusion from coastal regions
    B. Leaks from pipes
    C. Agricultural runoff
    D. Leaks from waste disposal sites

22. The phrase *natural recharge* refers to   22.____

    A. the recovery of a species from an event or trend that has lowered its population
    B. ionizing radiation in the environment from natural sources
    C. the replenishment of aquifers through precipitation and percolation
    D. the conversion of solar energy into food

23. Which of the following methods of agricultural inter-planting involves the planting of crops   23.____
    and trees together?

    A. Polyvarietal cultivation
    B. Intercropping
    C. Polyculture
    D. Alley cropping

24. The carrying capacity of a given area is determined by each of the following factors   24.____
    EXCEPT

    A. species diversity
    B. the availability of energy
    C. accumulation of waste products and their means of disposal
    D. interactions among organisms

25. Which of the following compounds is most strongly implicated in the ozone reduction of the upper atmosphere?   25.____

   A. Methane
   B. Nitrogen compound
   C. Peroxyacyl nitrates (PANs)
   D. Chlorofluorocarbon (CFC)

KEY (CORRECT ANSWERS)

1. B		11. C	
2. C		12. D	
3. D		13. C	
4. A		14. D	
5. D		15. D	
6. B		16. B	
7. B		17. B	
8. C		18. D	
9. D		19. B	
10. C		20. B	

21. C
22. C
23. D
24. A
25. C

TEST 2

DIRECTIONS: Each question or incomplete statement is followed by several suggested answers or completions. Select the one that BEST answers the question or completes the statement. *PRINT THE LETTER OF THE CORRECT ANSWER IN THE SPACE AT THE RIGHT.*

1. A stream where flow is maintained during the dry season by groundwater seepage into the channel is described as   1.____

    A. influent
    B. dry-charged
    C. effluent
    D. artesian

2. The ability of a species to produce offspring is referred to as its   2.____

    A. biotic potential
    B. fecundity
    C. potency
    D. fertility

3. _____ cost is the term for the harmful social effect, not included in the good's market price, of producing and using an economic good.   3.____

    A. External   B. True   C. Hidden   D. Full

4. In general, the biggest problem associated with the continued application of traditional pesticides is   4.____

    A. the harmful effects of these compounds on soil composition
    B. the collateral killing of natural predators or parasites that may have been maintaining a pest species at a reasonable level
    C. the development of genetic resistance by pest organisms
    D. providing the opportunity for new, unanticipated pests

5. Factors which tend to determine the success of a species more than any other are known as _____ factor.   5.____

    A. speciation
    B. biotic
    C. intraspecific
    D. limiting

6. Which of the following alternatives to gasoline involves no vehicle emissions?   6.____

    A. Solar-hydrogen
    B. Methanol
    C. Compressed natural gas
    D. Ethanol

7. Which of the following compounds are most likely to be biologically amplified as they move through the food chain?   7.____

    A. Nitrates
    B. Polychlorinated biphenyls (PCBs)
    C. Carbamates
    D. Peroxyacyl nitrates (PANs)

8. The *second* green revolution in global agriculture, begun around 1967, introduced the practice of   8.____

    A. increasing the intensity and frequency of cropping
    B. developing and planting monocultures of selectively bred or genetically engineered high-yield varieties of staple crops

C. lavishing fertilizer, pesticides, and water on crops to produce high yields
D. planting fast-growing dwarf varieties of rice and wheat in subtropical climates

9. For the prey in a predator-prey relationship, the most likely benefit is

   A. lower mortality rate
   B. learned stealth
   C. selection for quicker, healthier, and more fit individuals
   D. maintenance of abundant food sources

10. Which of the following are most likely to eat phytoplankton?

    A. Zooplankton
    B. Shrimp
    C. Fish
    D. Benthic organisms

11. Intraspecific competition occurs when

    A. one biome begins to overlap with another
    B. members of two or more species try to use the same limited resources in an ecosystem
    C. two populations in an ecosystem both reach their carrying capacity at the same time
    D. two or more individual organisms of a single species try to use the same limited resources in an ecosystem

12. Which of the following is/are direct sources of nitrogen for plants?
    I. Atmospheric nitrogen
    II. Ammonia
    III. Nitrates
    IV. Nitrites

    The CORRECT answer is:

    A. I only
    B. I, II
    C. II, III
    D. II, III, IV

13. Which of the following are NOT typically tertiary consumers?

    A. Hawks
    B. Snakes
    C. Lions
    D. Sharks

14. Approximately what percentage of the earth's surface is currently threatened with desertification?

    A. 10
    B. 20
    C. 33
    D. 50

15. What is the term for a region characterized by a particular aggregate of landforms, climate, and geomorphic history?

    A. Biome
    B. Niche
    C. Ecozone
    D. Physiographic province

16. Next to the oceans, most of the earth's water is contained in

    A. freshwater lakes
    B. ice caps and glaciers
    C. rivers and streams
    D. underground aquifers

17. Which of the following air pollutants is produced by tobacco smoke?   17._____

    A. Particulates   B. Hydrocarbons
    C. Carbon monoxide   D. Nitrogen compounds

18. The injection of water into an oil well to force out crude oil is most often referred to as   18._____
    _____ recovery.

    A. primary   B. secondary
    C. tertiary   D. enhanced

19. What is the term used to name the algae, animals, and fungi that remain attached at the   19._____
    bottom of moving streams and rivers?

    A. Submergents   B. Phytoplankton
    C. Limnus   D. Periphyton

20. Which of the following United States government lands are managed under the principle   20._____
    of restricted use?
        I.   National Wilderness Preservation Systems
        II. National Parks
        III. National Wildlife Refuges
        IV. National Forests
    The CORRECT answer is:

    A. I, II   B. I, III   C. II, III   D. III, IV

21. Which of the following pollutants poses a particular risk to the human brain?   21._____

    A. Zinc   B. Iodine   C. Mercury   D. Selenium

22. Which of the following is NOT a practice involved in the strategy of integrated pest management?   22._____

    A. The use of natural enemies of pests, including parasites, diseases, and predators
    B. No-till or low-till agriculture
    C. The planting of a greater diversity of crops
    D. The application of broad-spectrum herbicides rather than *magic bullet* herbicides

23. Which of the following CFC alternatives involve the fewest risks and/or disadvantages?   23._____

    A. Hydrocarbons   B. Ammonia
    C. Terpenes   D. Water/steam

24. Which of the following are most clearly *K-strategists*?   24._____

    A. Maple trees   B. Spiders
    C. Bears   D. Rabbits

25. The term *indirect deforestation* refers to the loss of trees through   25._____

    A. land clearings for residential or commercial development
    B. pollution or disease
    C. land clearings for agriculture
    D. watershed erosion

KEY (CORRECT ANSWERS)

1. C
2. A
3. A
4. C
5. D

6. A
7. B
8. D
9. C
10. A

11. D
12. C
13. B
14. B
15. D

16. B
17. C
18. B
19. D
20. A

21. C
22. D
23. C
24. C
25. B

EXAMINATION SECTION
TEST 1

DIRECTIONS: Each question or incomplete statement is followed by several suggested answers or completions. Select the one that BEST answers the question or completes the statement. *PRINT THE LETTER OF THE CORRECT ANSWER IN THE SPACE AT THE RIGHT.*

1. Generally, when energy passes from one trophic level to another in the food chain or food web, about _____ % of the usable energy is transferred. 1.____
   A. 10   B. 20   C. 33   D. 50

2. Of the following organic elements, which is the most unreactive? 2.____
   A. Oxygen   B. Carbon   C. Nitrogen   D. Hydrogen

3. The *first law of human ecology* states that 3.____
   A. uncontrolled population growth is the greatest threat to the planet's ecological integrity
   B. one cannot get more energy out of something than is put into it
   C. nature exists for all the earth's species
   D. any intrusion into nature has numerous effects

4. Which of the following federal laws established the requirement that all major federal projects that might affect the quality of the human environment be preceded by an evaluation of the project and its potential impact on the environment? 4.____
   A. Multiple Use Sustained Yield Act of 1968
   B. National Environmental Policy Act (NEPA) of 1969
   C. Resource Conservation and Recovery Act of 1976
   D. Comprehensive Environmental Response, Compensation, and Liability Act (CERCLA) of 1986

5. What is the term for a land area that delivers water, sediment, and dissolved substances to a major stream or river via small streams? 5.____
   A. Riparian zone   B. Divide
   C. Buffer zone   D. Watershed

6. Of the 7 billion tons of carbon that were released into the atmosphere throughout the 1980s, only about 3.2 billion tons remained in the atmosphere. The current hypothesis among scientists is that the bulk of this *missing carbon* is 6.____
   A. dissolved in freshwater resources
   B. stored in forests of the northern hemisphere
   C. locked into agricultural runoff
   D. dissolved in the oceans

7. What is the term for noxious, mineralized liquids that are capable of transmitting bacterial pollutants? 7.____
   A. Effluent   B. Leachate   C. Tailings   D. Dioxin

8. Which of the following statements about pesticides is generally FALSE?

    A. The health risks of pesticides are negligible compared with their health benefits.
    B. They remain fairly immobile once applied.
    C. They work faster and better than alternatives.
    D. They lower food costs.

9. A lake with a low supply of plant nutrients is described as

    A. atrophic   B. mesotrophic   C. oligotrophic   D. eutrophic

10. Which of the following compounds is associated with the earliest stage in the carbon-silicate cycle?

    A. Carbonic acid   B. Hydrocarbon
    C. Calcium carbonate   D. Bicarbonate ion

11. Probably the most important step toward slowing the global warming phenomenon would be to

    A. more carefully use nitrogen-containing fertilizers
    B. increase the overall efficiency of energy utilization
    C. completely ban the use of all CFCs
    D. plant multitudes of trees to help remove CO_2 from the atmosphere

12. Which of the following is NOT a product of aerobic respiration?

    A. Carbon dioxide   B. Energy
    C. Water   D. Glucose

13. Biological diversity is universally thought to consist of each of the following concepts EXCEPT _____ diversity.

    A. climatic   B. genetic   C. habitat   D. species

14. When a material is removed from the earth's surface or subsurface by mining, dredging, quarrying, and excavation, the unwanted rock and other waste materials produced are referred to as

    A. gangue   B. tailings   C. spoils   D. substrata

15. Each of the following elements is found in every living thing on the planet and is recycled when an organism dies EXCEPT

    A. calcium   B. phosphorus   C. nitrogen   D. hydrogen

16. The concept that the growth or survival of a population is directly related to the life requirement that is in least supply, and not to a combination of factors, is known as the

    A. law of succession   B. competitive exclusion principle
    C. law of tolerance   D. law of the minimum

17. Which of the following is an example of a cosmopolitan species?

    A. Monterey cypress   B. Moose
    C. Polar bear   D. Humans

18. The term *overburden* refers to

    A. an excess of the threshold of stress – from chemical fertilizers and natural depletion – that an agricultural soil can tolerate
    B. the layer of soil and rock overlying a mineral deposit
    C. the point at which water can no longer flow from one underground pore space to another
    D. the point at which an ecosystem's resources can no longer sustain the current population of a species

19. Nearly all the carbon stored in the earth's lithosphere exists as

    A. methane
    B. igneous rocks
    C. metamorphic rocks
    D. sedimentary rocks

20. What is the term for any close, long-lasting physical relationship between two different species of organisms?

    A. Affinity   B. Commensalism   C. Synergy   D. Symbiosis

21. The primary component of industrial smog is

    A. ozone
    B. sulfur dioxide
    C. chlorofluorocarbons (CFCs)
    D. carbon monoxide

22. In flowing streams, which of the following factors contribute to the fact that downstream ecosystems generally contain less dissolved oxygen than those further upstream?
    I. Slower flow
    II. Thinner tree canopy
    III. Lower altitude
    IV. Agricultural runoff
    The CORRECT answer is:

    A. I, II   B. III, IV   C. I, II, IV   D. II, III, IV

23. Which of the following factors would tend to increase species diversity in an ecosystem?

    A. Frequent and extreme disturbance
    B. The introduction of exotic species
    C. The middle stages of ecological succession
    D. Geographic isolation

24. Of the following methods for removing particulates from the exhaust gases of electric power and industrial plants, a(n) _____ is also useful for reducing sulfur dioxide emissions.

    A. wet scrubber
    B. baghouse filter
    C. cyclone separator
    D. electrostatic precipitator

25. What is the term for the process of separating an ore mineral from waste mineral material?

    A. Beneficiation
    B. Gangue
    C. Eutrophication
    D. Tailing

KEY (CORRECT ANSWERS)

1.	A	11.	B
2.	C	12.	D
3.	D	13.	A
4.	B	14.	C
5.	D	15.	A
6.	D	16.	D
7.	B	17.	D
8.	B	18.	B
9.	C	19.	D
10.	A	20.	D

21. B
22. C
23. C
24. A
25. A

TEST 2

DIRECTIONS: Each question or incomplete statement is followed by several suggested answers or completions. Select the one that BEST answers the question or completes the statement. *PRINT THE LETTER OF THE CORRECT ANSWER IN THE SPACE AT THE RIGHT.*

1. Which of the following is a term for a stage in ecological succession?

    A. Trophic level   B. Sere   C. Echelon   D. Steppe

2. In general, as the amount of organic waste in a body of water increases, the

    A. biological oxygen demand (BOD) increases
    B. greater the risk of oligotrophy
    C. biological oxygen demand (BOD) decreases
    D. risk of die-off increases

3. According to the National Academy of Sciences and most other members of the scientific community, the most important priority in adopting a low-waste approach should be to

    A. recycle and compost as much waste as possible
    B. reduce the production of waste and pollution
    C. treat or incinerate waste that can't otherwise be prevented or transformed
    D. reuse as many things as possible

4. Which of the following is not a product of the nitrogen fixation process?

    A. Molecular nitrogen   B. Ammonia
    C. Nitrate ion   D. Amino acids

5. Of the following, the most important group of rock-forming minerals are the

    A. pyroxines   B. carbonates   C. phosphates   D. silicates

6. The active decomposition zone of a stream is associated with

    A. waterborne pathogens
    B. a minimum dissolved oxygen content
    C. eutrophication
    D. reduced biological oxygen demand (BOD)

7. The third layer of the atmosphere, found above the stratosphere, is the

    A. thermosphere   B. mesosphere   C. troposphere   D. ionosphere

8. Which of the following types of pesticides tend to be most persistent in the environment?

    A. Soil sterilants   B. Botanicals
    C. Chlorinated hydrocarbons   D. Carbamates

9. Which of the following pollutants is most likely to effect changes in the distribution of wildlife population?

    A. Asbestos   B. Arsenic
    C. Nitrogen oxides   D. Fluoride

10. The primary stage in oil field production typically recovers about _____ % of the oil contained within the reservoir.

    A. 10   B. 25   C. 50   D. 75

11. A system's ability to maintain favorable internal conditions, despite changes in external conditions, is specifically known as

    A. homogeneity   B. constancy
    C. homeostasis   D. inertia

12. Which of the following international environmental summits resulted in agreements to reduce the air pollutants that destroy stratospheric ozone?

    A. Antarctic Treaty of 1961
    B. 1979 Conference on Long-Range Transboundary Air Pollution
    C. Montreal Protocol of 1987
    D. U.N. Earth Summit of 1992

13. Which of the following is a general term for all the organisms of all species living in an area or region?

    A. Biota   B. Fauna   C. Biome   D. Biomass

14. Which of the following is NOT a step described in the traditional demographic transition model of human populations?

    A. Initially, countries have an unstable population with a low birth rate and a low death rate.
    B. Improved economic and social conditions bring about a period of rapid growth.
    C. As countries become industrialized, birth rates drop as people make use of contraceptives.
    D. Eventually, birth rates and deaths become balanced.

15. As a pollutant, which site on the human body will cadmium affect to the greatest degree?

    A. Bones   B. Heart   C. Liver   D. Skin

16. Of the topsoil that erodes away each day in the United States, what percentage comes from land that is used to graze cattle or to raise crops to feed cattle?

    A. 20   B. 45   C. 60   D. 85

17. Which of the following is the clearest example of a primary consumer?

    A. Pine tree   B. Wolf   C. Deer   D. Trout

18. In the control of industrial pollution, the scrubbing process is used primarily to remove _____ from gases emitted from power plants burning coal.

    A. calcium   B. carbon   C. lead   D. sulfur

19. Of the following, the greatest drawback to conservation-tillage farming is

    A. the potential for increased pesticide requirements with certain crops
    B. greater overall expense
    C. lower overall yield
    D. the potential for compaction of soil

20. Which of the following is NOT a commonly applied definition of biomass?

    A. Dry weight of all organic matter in plants and animals in an ecosystem
    B. Plant materials and animal wastes used as fuel
    C. Zone of the earth where life is found
    D. Organic matter produced by plants and other photo-synthetic producers

21. The kind of ecological succession that occurs after the destruction or disturbance of an existing ecosystem is known as _____ succession.

    A. primary   B. secondary
    C. pioneer   D. serai

22. Species that are introduced into a new area by human action are described as

    A. hostile   B. endemic   C. alien   D. exotic

23. Which of the following pollutants is caused by the incomplete burning of fossil fuels?

    A. Particulates   B. Hydrocarbons
    C. Sulfur dioxide   D. Nitrogen compounds

24. An interaction of two or more factors or processes, in which the combined effect is greater than the sum of their separate effects, is described as

    A. synergistic   B. entropic
    C. alchemistic   D. post-threshold

25. In the carbon cycle, carbon frequently enters the atmosphere through each of the following processes or events EXCEPT

    A. the respiration of living things
    B. fires that burn organic compounds
    C. winds that lift small sediments
    D. diffusion from the ocean

KEY (CORRECT ANSWERS)

1. B
2. A
3. B
4. A
5. D

6. B
7. B
8. C
9. D
10. B

11. C
12. C
13. A
14. A
15. B

16. D
17. C
18. D
19. A
20. C

21. B
22. D
23. B
24. A
25. C

EXAMINATION SECTION
TEST 1

DIRECTIONS: Each question or incomplete statement is followed by several suggested answers or completions. Select the one that BEST answers the question or completes the statement. *PRINT THE LETTER OF THE CORRECT ANSWER IN THE SPACE AT THE RIGHT.*

1. In the course of his inspection of a plant, a sanitarian obtains information about a process which he thinks would be useful to a friend engaged in a similar business.
   Of the following, the MOST advisable course of action for him to take is to

   A. consider such information confidential and not disclose it
   B. consider such information not confidential and, therefore, disclose it to his friend
   C. give his friend the information, but not disclose its source
   D. give his friend the information, pretending that it is his own idea

2. Assume that, as a sanitarian, you have received an order from a person of high authority in the Department of Health. This order conflicts with instructions which you have received from your immediate supervisor.
   Of the following, the MOST advisable action for you to take FIRST is to

   A. carry out the order given you by higher authority
   B. inform your supervisor of the situation
   C. proceed according to your supervisor's instructions
   D. send a written memorandum to the person who gave you the order, indicating the conflict with your immediate supervisor's instructions

3. Of the following statements concerning reports prepared by a sanitarian, the one which is LEAST valid is:

   A. A case report submitted by a sanitarian should contain factual material to support conclusions made
   B. An extremely detailed report may be of less value than a brief report giving the essential facts
   C. Highly technical language should be avoided as far as possible in preparing a report to be used at a court trial
   D. The position of the important facts in a report does not influence the emphasis placed on them by the reader

4. Assume that, as a sanitarian, you are to leave the restaurant after having concluded an inspection of the premises. However, the operator begins a detailed story concerning his business experiences.
   Of the following, the MOST advisable course of action for you to take is to

   A. leave immediately to avoid being delayed by listening to the story
   B. listen for a few minutes and then excuse yourself on the ground that you have other duties
   C. listen quietly to what he has to say, but be noncommittal in making replies
   D. tell the operator that the job of sanitarian does not permit indulgence in personal relationships with operators

17

5. Suppose that a story concerning an investigation conducted by the Department of Health has appeared in the newspapers. A reporter approaches a sanitarian and asks for details concerning this investigation.
Of the following, the MOST advisable way for the sanitarian to handle the situation is to

   A. give the reporter complete information regarding the investigation
   B. refer the reporter to the official of the department responsible for public relations
   C. refuse to speak to the reporter
   D. tell the reporter to make his own investigation of the matter

6. The operator of an establishment tells you that he intends to register a complaint against you, the sanitarian, with the Department of Health. He claims that you are impeding his operations because you insist upon a minute inspection of every piece of equipment. You feel that your methods are justified.
Of the following, the MOST advisable course of action for you to take is to

   A. continue the inspection, and ignore the complaint because you feel that your methods are correct
   B. continue the inspection, but tell the operator that owners of similar establishments do not complain concerning the same type of inspection
   C. explain the reasons for your actions to the operator and inform him that he has the right to complain if he wishes
   D. try to cut down on some of the details of the inspection in order to maintain a good relationship with the operator

7. Assume that, as a sanitarian, you are inspecting the premises of a certain establishment. The owner tells you of his disagreement with certain provisions of the new Health Code which affect his business.
Of the following, the MOST advisable course of action for you to take is to

   A. tell him that most such complaints are groundless
   B. tell him that your workload does not permit you to spend time discussing the new Health Code
   C. tell him to make his complaint in person to the Department of Health
   D. try to explain the reasons for the inclusion of these provisions

8. Suppose that, as a sanitarian, you realize that you have made an error in a report that has been forwarded to another unit. You know that this error is not likely to be discovered for some time.
Of the following, the MOST advisable course of action for you to take is to

   A. approach the supervisor of the other unit on an informal basis and ask him to correct the error
   B. say nothing about it since most likely one error will not invalidate the entire report
   C. tell your supervisor immediately that you have made an error so that it may be corrected, if necessary
   D. wait until the error is discovered and then admit that you have made it

9. Suppose that you have become friendly with one of the other sanitarians in your unit. You notice that recently he has been doing very poor work and you know that the rest of the staff is aware of the situation.
Of the following, the MOST advisable course of action for you to take is to

A. seek an opportunity to speak privately to your friend and ask if you can help in any way
B. speak to the other members of the staff when you have an opportunity, and try to minimize the situation
C. speak to your supervisor and tell him that he ought to transfer this man to another unit
D. tell your friend that you are willing to share some of his workload for a while

10. Assume that, as a sanitarian, you realize that you have unjustly reprimanded the owner of an establishment while making an inspection.
Of the following, the MOST advisable course of action for you to take is to

A. admit your mistake and apologize to the owner
B. attempt to justify the reprimand on some other basis
C. ignore the matter in order to maintain your authority
D. overlook some other offense you may notice

10.____

Question 11.

DIRECTIONS: Question 11 is to be answered SOLELY on the basis of the following passage from the Health Code.

A drug or device shall be deemed to be misbranded:

1. If any word, statement, or other information required by this article to appear on the label or labeling is not prominently placed thereon with such conspicuousness, as compared with other words, statements, designs or emblems in the labeling, and in such terms as to render it likely to be read and understood by the ordinary individual under customary conditions of purchase and use; or,

2. If it is a drug and is not designated solely by a name recognized in an official compendium unless its label bears the common or usual name of the drug, if it has one, and, if it is fabricated from two or more ingredients, the common or usual name of each active ingredient, including the kind and quantity by percentage or amount of any alcohol; or,

3. Unless its labeling bears adequate directions for use, except that a drug or device may be exempted from this requirement by the Commissioner when he finds that it is not necessary for the protection of the public health, and such adequate warnings against use in those pathological conditions or by children where its use may be dangerous to health, or against unsafe dosage or methods or duration of administration or application, in such manner and form, as are necessary for the protection of users.

11. According to the above passage, the LEAST accurate of the following statements is:

A. Certain drugs must have labels which give their names as found in an official compendium
B. Drugs or devices are not necessarily misbranded if their labels carry warnings against use in certain pathological conditions
C. Labels on drugs liable to deterioration must state the precautions necessary to prevent deterioration
D. Required information on a drug label should be at least as conspicuous as other statements on the label

11.____

Questions 12-13.

DIRECTIONS: Questions 12 and 13 are to be answered SOLELY on the basis of the following passage from the Health Code.

(a) The Commissioner shall not consent to the use or proposed use of a food additive if the data before him:
(1) fail to establish that the proposed use of the additive under the conditions of use specified will be safe; or,
(2) show that the proposed use of the additive would otherwise result in adulteration or in misbranding of food within the meaning of this Code.

(b) If, in the opinion of the Commissioner, based on the data before him, a tolerance limitation is required in order to assure that the proposed use of an additive will be safe, the Commissioner:
(1) shall not fix such tolerance limitation at a level higher than he finds to be reasonably required to accomplish the physical or other technical effect for which such additive is intended; and,
(2) shall not consent to the proposed use of the additive if he finds that the data do not establish that such use would accomplish the intended physical or other technical effect.

(c) In determining whether a proposed use of a food additive is safe, the Commissioner shall consider among other relevant factors:
(1) the probable consumption of the additive and of any substance formed in the food because of the use of the additive; and,
(2) the cumulative effect of such additive in the diet of man or animals.

12. If the data indicate that the proposed use of a food additive will be safe if the amount added is limited to 5 milligrams per gram of the food, the Commissioner shall fix the tolerance limitation at

A. 5 milligrams per gram of the food
B. 4 milligrams per gram of the food if this is the amount that can be expected to produce the desired effect
C. less than 5 but more than 4 milligrams per gram of the food if 4 milligrams is the amount that can be expected to produce the desired effect
D. less than 5 milligrams per gram of the food

13. According to the above passage, the LEAST accurate of the following statements is:

A. Some food additives may, in some cases, be considered as adulterants
B. The Commissioner should consider all relevant factors in determining whether the proposed use of a food additive is safe
C. The Commissioner may not prohibit the use of an additive if the data show that its use is safe within certain tolerance limitations
D. The Commissioner may prohibit the use of an additive even if the data indicate that its use would be safe within certain tolerance limitations

14. Of the following, a LIKELY reason for the inclusion of section (b)(2) given above is that 14._____
    A. food additives used within their tolerance limitations are likely to be unsafe
    B. producers may tend to add more than the safe amount if the tolerance limitation does not permit the accomplishment of the intended physical or other technical effect
    C. the probable consumption of the additive cannot be determined if it does not accomplish the intended physical or other technical effect
    D. use of a food additive that does not accomplish the intended physical or other technical effect is uneconomical

Questions 15-16.

DIRECTIONS: Questions 15 and 16 are to be answered SOLELY on the basis of the following passage from the Health Code.

The new Health Code governs such aspects of the food industry as pertain to cleanliness of apparatus, equipment, and utensils used in the preparation and service of food and sanitation of food establishment premises.

This revision marks a considerable shift in emphasis from detailed specific standards to broad performance standards and the imposition of greater obligation on industry to carry out well-formulated inspection procedures under its own direction and under continuing supervision of the Department. The emphasis is on clean and sanitary food products produced, sold or served in clean and sanitary food establishments.

The emphasis on generalized performance standards serves the important purpose of encouraging, through less restrictive regulations, the development of new processes in food sanitation and food manufacture. The advances in food technology practices, new chemical aids and new sanitary designs of machinery, have already pointed the way to getting the job done better and without the need for restrictive detailed regulations. This article is not only designed to permit progress of this kind to the fullest, but it also reflects the view that such industry growth should receive constant stimulation so that there is less need for official policing and more and more self-sanitation and self-supervision.

15. According to the above passage, the new Health Code 15._____
    A. requires detailed specific standards rather than broad performance standards
    B. is intended to provide for ultimate complete self-supervision by the food industry
    C. places less emphasis on self-inspection than on generalized performance standards
    D. is designed to take cognizance of the effects of new developments on food industry practices

16. According to the above passage, the new Health Code does NOT 16._____
    A. consider continued supervision of the food industry by the Department to be of great importance
    B. consider that advances in food technology indicate the need for less restrictive regulations

C. emphasize coercion but seeks voluntary compliance by the food industry
D. obligate the food industry to carry out well-formulated inspection procedures under its own direction

Questions 17-18.

DIRECTIONS: Questions 17 and 18 are to be answered SOLELY on the basis of the following passage.

The beginnings of hygiene can be traced back to antiquity in the sanitary laws of the Hebrews. Preventive medicine began with the first primitive idea of contagion. Even in the time when epidemics were explained as due to the wrath of the gods or visitations of evil spirits, it was observed that certain illnesses apparently spread from person to person. Gradually, the idea of contagiousness was associated with a number of diseases. Fracastorium, in his book, DE CONTAGIONE, published in 1554, proposed a classification of diseases into those which were contagious and those which were not. For three centuries following this publication, the medical profession was divided into two camps: the non-contagionists, who believed that the causative agents of epidemic disease were inanimate and gaseous in nature and associated with emanations from decomposing organic matter, effluvia, and miasma; and the much smaller group, the contagionists, who identified contagiousness with germs of some kind.

Looking backward, this confusion is understandable. That some diseases were contagious was fairly obvious, but some apparently arose spontaneously without a traceable source. The confusion was finally resolved in the latter part of the nineteenth century by the work of Pasteur, Koch, and their followers. The causative relationship of specific microorganisms for one after another of the infectious diseases was established and the part played by carriers, missed cases, common water and food supplies, arthropod vectors, and animal reservoirs in transmission was gradually elucidated.

17. The above passage IMPLIES that

   A. all infectious diseases were highly contagious
   B. the contagionists of the early 19th century had identified the specific microorganisms causing certain diseases
   C. the role of animal reservoirs contributed to the confusion which once existed concerning disease transmission
   D. the sanitary laws of the ancient Hebrews show that they had some scientific knowledge of the causes of disease

18. According to the above passage, the MOST accurate of the following statements is:

   A. Fracastorius believed that all diseases could be caused by miasma
   B. It is still believed by scientists that certain infectious diseases arise spontaneously
   C. Nothing was accomplished in disease prevention until the germ theory was established
   D. Preventive medicine was practiced to some extent in early times even though epidemics may have been attributed to evil spirits

Questions 19-20.

DIRECTIONS: Questions 19 and 20 are to be answered SOLELY on the basis of the following paragraph.

Microorganisms are living things so small that they can be seen only with the aid of a microscope. They are widely distributed in nature and are responsible for many physical and chemical changes of importance to the life of plants, of animals, and of human beings. Altogether too many people believe that all *microbes* or *germs* are harmful, and that they are an entirely undesirable group of living things. While it is true that some microorganisms produce disease, the great majority of them do not. In fact, the activities of these hosts of non-disease-producing microorganisms make possible the continued existence of plants and animals on the earth. In addition, many kinds of microorganisms are used in industries to manufacture products of great value to man. But the activities of non-disease-producing microorganisms are not always desirable. Fabrics and fibers may be rotted, fermentation processes may be upset by undesirable organisms and other harmful effects may occur. From a practical point of view, we are interested in the microorganisms because of the things that they do and the physical and chemical changes which they produce. Also, we are interested in ways and means to control undesirable organisms and to put the useful ones to work; but a study of the activities and the means for control of microorganisms must be based upon knowledge of their nature and life processes.

19. The one of the following which is the MOST suitable title for the above paragraph is   19.____

    A. BACTERIA CAN BE USEFUL
    B. MICROORGANISMS AND THE PUBLIC HEALTH SANITARIAN
    C. THE CONTROL OF MICROBES
    D. THE RELATIONSHIP OF MICROORGANISMS TO MAN AND HIS ENVIRONMENT

20. According to the above paragraph, the MOST accurate of the following statements is: 20.____

    A. All non-disease-producing microorganisms are beneficial to mankind
    B. *Microbes* or *germs* are terms which are synonymous with *bacteria*
    C. The activities of useful bacteria need no controls
    D. Without microorganisms, life on earth would be virtually impossible

KEY (CORRECT ANSWERS)

1.	A	11.	C
2.	B	12.	B
3.	D	13.	C
4.	B	14.	B
5.	B	15.	D
6.	C	16.	C
7.	D	17.	C
8.	C	18.	D
9.	A	19.	D
10.	A	20.	D

TEST 2

DIRECTIONS: Each question or incomplete statement is followed by several suggested answers or completions. Select the one that BEST answers the question or completes the statement. *PRINT THE LETTER OF THE CORRECT ANSWER IN THE SPACE AT THE RIGHT.*

1. Solutions to which relatively large amounts of strong acid or base can be added with ONLY SLIGHT resulting change in pH are called _____ solutions.

    A. buffered   B. molar   C. normal   D. standard

2. Of the following statements concerning isotopes, the one which is INCORRECT is that isotopes of a given element have

    A. similar chemical properties
    B. the same atomic number
    C. the same atomic weight
    D. the same nuclear charge

3. Nuclei of atoms are considered to be composed of

    A. neutrons and protons
    B. photons and electrons
    C. positrons and neutrons
    D. protons and electrons

4. *Dry Ice* is solid

    A. ammonia
    B. carbolic acid
    C. carbon dioxide
    D. freon

5. The pH of a solution in which the apparent hydrogen ion concentration is equal to 1×10^{-8} moles per liter is

    A. 2   B. 4   C. 6   D. 8

6. Substances in solutions which change color at a particular pH are termed

    A. catalysts
    B. desiccants
    C. indicators
    D. mordants

7. The amount of 2.0 N KOH required to neutralize 40 ml. of 0.5 N HCl is _____ ml.

    A. 2   B. 4   C. 5   D. 10

8. The term *anion* refers to a

    A. *negatively* charged electrode
    B. *negatively* charged ion
    C. *positively* charged electrode
    D. *positively* charged ion

9. If the concentration of a salt solution is given as 0.7243 grams per liter, it may also be expressed as _____ grams per liter.

    A. 7.243×10^{-2}
    B. 72.43×10^{-1}
    C. 72.43×10^{-2}
    D. 724.3×10^{-2}

10. Invertase is a type of

    A. carbohydrate B. enzyme
    C. fat   D. protein

11. An enzyme that acts upon starches is said to be

    A. aminolytic   B. amylolytic
    C. lipolytic   D. proteolytic

12. The structural formula $H_2N-\underset{H}{\overset{H}{C}}-C\overset{O}{\underset{OH}{}}$ represents a(n)

    A. ketone   B. alcohol
    C. amino acid   D. ester

13. The one of the following which is a PRODUCT of the saponification of a fat is

    A. glycerol   B. glycine   C. lecithin   D. sterol

14. Synthetic detergents can be used INSTEAD of natural soaps because both

    A. are organic compounds
    B. have the same chemical composition
    C. lower the surface tension of water
    D. raise the surface tension of water

15. A Bourdon gage is used to measure

    A. electrical resistance   B. gas pressure
    C. internal diameters   D. relative humidity

16. A specific gravity bottle weighs 150 g when empty, 250 g when filled with water, and 385 g when filled with another liquid.
    The specific gravity of the liquid is MOST NEARLY

    A. 1.67   B. 2.35   C. 2.57   D. 3.85

17. At sea level, the number of degrees between the freezing point and the boiling point of water on the Centigrade temperature scale is

    A. 32   B. 100   C. 180   D. 212

18. The general gas law for a given mass of gas, where P stands for pressure, V stands for volume, and T stands for absolute temperature may be stated as

    A. P = KVT   B. PK = VT   C. PT = KV   D. PV = KT

19. If a mercury column barometer is constructed with a tube twice the diameter of a standard barometer, the reading will be _____ that of the standard barometer.

    A. one-fourth of   B. one-half of
    C. twice   D. the same as

20. The watt is a unit of electrical

    A. current
    B. inductance
    C. potential
    D. power

21. Bacteria are classified with the

    A. Bryophytes
    B. Protozoa
    C. Pteridophytes
    D. Thallophytes

22. The scientific name of a certain microorganism is Clostridium butyricum. The second word of this name indicates the

    A. class   B. genus   C. phylum   D. species

23. Suppose that 100 ml of a water sample are added to 1900 ml of dilution water, and that 1 ml of this dilution is added to 49 ml of dilution water.
    The dilution of the original water sample in the second mixture is 1:

    A. 900   B. 950   C. 1000   D. 1250

24. Spheroid shaped bacteria which look like chains of beads under the microscope are known as

    A. sarcinas
    B. spirilla
    C. staphylococci
    D. streptococci

25. In addition to alcohol, the fermentation of glucose by yeast yields

    A. carbon dioxide
    B. citric acid
    C. hydrogen
    D. oxygen

KEY (CORRECT ANSWERS)

1. A		11. B	
2. C		12. C	
3. A		13. A	
4. C		14. C	
5. D		15. B	
6. C		16. B	
7. D		17. B	
8. B		18. D	
9. C		19. D	
10. B		20. D	

21. D
22. D
23. C
24. D
25. A

TEST 3

DIRECTIONS: Each question or incomplete statement is followed by several suggested answers or completions. Select the one that BEST answers the question or completes the statement. *PRINT THE LETTER OF THE CORRECT ANSWER IN THE SPACE AT THE RIGHT.*

1. The one of the following which is NOT an antibiotic is
    A. actinomycin
    B. trypsin
    C. streptothricin
    D. tyrothricin

2. Vaccination confers _____ acquired immunity.
    A. *active* artificially
    B. *active* naturally
    C. *passive* artificially
    D. *passive* naturally

3. The one of the following which is NOT used as a disinfectant or antiseptic is
    A. ethyl acetate
    B. phenol
    C. potassium permanganate
    D. silver nitrate

4. The vector responsible for the transmission of yellow fever is the
    A. flea
    B. louse
    C. mosquito
    D. tick

5. Typhus fever is caused by microorganisms of the genus
    A. Escherichia
    B. Proteus
    C. Rickettsia
    D. Salmonella

6. The one of the following diseases which is caused by a virus is
    A. encephalitis
    B. malaria
    C. Q fever
    D. tetanus

7. The one of the following diseases which is considered to be infectious is
    A. angina pectoria
    B. diabetes
    C. glaucoma
    D. psittacosis

8. The one of the following diseases in which rats do NOT act as intermediate hosts is
    A. amoebic dysentery
    B. endemic typhus
    C. plague
    D. Weil's disease

9. The Kahn test is used to diagnose
    A. gonorrhea
    B. syphilis
    C. tuberculosis
    D. typhoid fever

10. The one of the following BEST known for his work in connection with antibiotics is
    A. Löffler
    B. Rivers
    C. Waksman
    D. Welch

11. Of the following constituents of milk, the one which is present in the LEAST proportion is
    A. fat
    B. mineral ash
    C. protein
    D. sugar

27

12. Casein occurs in fresh milk in the form of a(n)

    A. colloidal solution
    B. foam
    C. emulsion
    D. true solution

13. One type of lactometer used for determining the specific gravity of milk is graduated from 0 to 29 degrees to indicate a certain range of specific gravity. Another type is graduated from 0 to 100 degrees to indicate the same range.
If the specific gravity is determined from the reading of the first type by the formula, $1 + \dfrac{\text{reading}}{1000}$, then the formula to be used with the second type is

    A. $1 + (\dfrac{\text{reading}}{1000} \times \dfrac{1}{.29})$
    B. $1 + (\dfrac{\text{reading}}{1000} \times .29)$
    C. $(\dfrac{\text{reading}}{1000} \times .29) - 1$
    D. $(\dfrac{\text{reading}}{1000} \times \dfrac{1}{.29}) - 1$

14. If milk is adulterated by the addition of water, its

    A. specific gravity will be decreased
    B. specific gravity will be increased
    C. relative fat content will be increased
    D. relative mineral content will be increased

15. The *Holding* method and the *High Temperature Short Time* method of milk pasteurization require, respectively, _____ minutes and _____ seconds.

    A. 15; 15   B. 15; 30   C. 30; 30   D. 30; 15

16. Of the following, the one which is NOT used for testing milk is the _____ test.

    A. methylene blue reduction
    B. phosphatase
    C. precipitin
    D. sediment

17. The one of the following which is ordinarily NOT considered to be a disease transmissible through milk is

    A. scarlet fever
    B. septic sore throat
    C. spotted fever
    D. brucellosis

18. The one of the following which would ordinarily NOT be used in sterilizing milk plant equipment is

    A. chlorine solution
    B. sodium fluoroacetate
    C. hot water
    D. live steam

19. The legal requirement for butter is that its butterfat content shall be NOT less than

    A. 95%   B. 90%   C. 85%   D. 80%

20. Of the following, the one which is COMMONLY used as a stabilizer for ice cream is

    A. albumin
    B. benzoic acid
    C. gelatin
    D. sucrose

21. Of the following, the one which is NOT a factor used in grading butter is

    A. body
    B. butterfat content
    C. color
    D. salt

22. When fortifying milk with vitamin D, the minimum number of vitamin D units required per quart is USUALLY

    A. 400
    B. 600
    C. 800
    D. 1000

23. Milk is USUALLY tested for adequacy of homogenization by

    A. allowing it to stand for 48 hours and then observing the percentage of butterfat which rises to the upper portion
    B. employing a modified Babcock test
    C. noting the time required for coagulation of the milk
    D. using a centrifuge

24. Rennet, used in cheese manufacture, is obtained

    A. by chemical synthesis
    B. from bacterial cultures
    C. from calves' stomachs
    D. from goats' milk

25. A *starter* used in making cheese is a(n)

    A. bacterial culture
    B. mechanical agitator
    C. enzyme
    D. organic acid

26. The term *process cheese* refers to cheese

    A. made by old European methods not readily duplicated in the United States
    B. made from one or more varieties of cheese which have been reworked into a mixture with a smooth texture
    C. which is manufactured by a patented method
    D. which is permitted to ripen for a considerable length of time

27. Curing preserves meat PRIMARILY because of the

    A. high temperatures at which the curing process is carried on
    B. low temperatures at which the curing process is carried on
    C. use of salt in fairly high concentration
    D. use of spices in low concentration

28. In commercial canning of low-acid food, appropriate *heat processing* is used in order to

    A. destroy spore-forming bacteria
    B. expel air and other gases from the product
    C. fix the natural color of the product
    D. remove raw flavors from the foods

29. Custard-filled baked goods are FREQUENTLY involved in cases of food poisoning primarily because

    A. harmful preservatives are sometimes used in custards
    B. many people are allergic to some of the ingredients used in custard
    C. the custard forms a good medium for growth of certain harmful bacteria
    D. the ingredients may be stale

30. An unsexed male chicken (usually under 10 months of age) is called a 30._____
    A. broiler B. capon C. fryer D. stag

KEY (CORRECT ANSWERS)

1.	B	16.	C
2.	A	17.	C
3.	A	18.	B
4.	C	19.	D
5.	C	20.	C
6.	A	21.	B
7.	D	22.	A
8.	A	23.	A
9.	B	24.	C
10.	C	25.	A
11.	B	26.	B
12.	A	27.	C
13.	B	28.	A
14.	A	29.	C
15.	D	30.	B

TEST 4

DIRECTIONS: Each question or incomplete statement is followed by several suggested answers or completions. Select the one that BEST answers the question or completes the statement. *PRINT THE LETTER OF THE CORRECT ANSWER IN THE SPACE AT THE RIGHT.*

1. An unopened can containing spoiled food which CANNOT be detected by its external appearance is called a

    A. flat sour
    B. flipper
    C. springer
    D. swell

    1.____

2. The one of the following which is usually NOT a factor considered in determining the grade of canned fruit is the

    A. color of the fruit
    B. density of the syrup
    C. texture of the fruit
    D. uniformity of size

    2.____

3. The term *marbling*, as used in connection with the grading of beef, refers to

    A. a hardened condition of the bones
    B. coarseness in the texture of the meat
    C. the external fat covering the meat
    D. the network of intramuscular fat visible in the cut surface of the meat

    3.____

4. Food poisoning is MOST likely to be caused by bacteria of the genus

    A. Neisseria
    B. Pasteurella
    C. Salmonella
    D. Treponema

    4.____

5. When candling eggs, the characteristic which indicates eggs of SUPERIOR quality is

    A. germ development
    B. large air cell
    C. slightly defined yolk outline
    D. weak white

    5.____

6. *Enriched bread* is thus designated because it contains added

    A. eggs
    B. minerals and vitamins
    C. shortening
    D. sugar

    6.____

7. Oysters may be involved in outbreaks of disease PRIMARILY because they may

    A. contain parasitic worms
    B. have been eaten while still immature
    C. have been taken from polluted waters
    D. have been transplanted to water containing less salt than the original bed

    7.____

8. The one of the following which is NOT a vitamin of the B complex is

    A. carotene
    B. pantothenic acid
    C. riboflavin
    D. thiamine

    8.____

9. The department that enforces the Federal Food, Drug, and Cosmetic Act is the Department of

   A. Agriculture
   B. Commerce
   C. Health, Education and Welfare
   D. the Interior

10. The CHIEF purpose for regulating the sale of barbiturates is to

    A. be able to check the amount of stock of barbiturates a dispenser has on hand
    B. be able to identify purchasers
    C. discourage their use and sale
    D. prevent their use by irresponsible persons

11. The one of the following diseases which is NOT considered to be transmissible through water is

    A. anthrax   B. bacillary dysentery
    C. cholera   D. typhoid fever

12. The one of the following which is NOT used as a coagulant in water purification is

    A. aluminum sulfate   B. ferric chloride
    C. ferric sulfate   D. sodium phosphate

13. Routine bacteriological examination of water tests for the presence of coliform organisms.
    This is done because

    A. absence of coliforms warrants the assumption that water-borne pathogens are absent
    B. the coliforms are the easiest to collect in a water sample
    C. the coliforms are the most highly pathogenic water-borne organisms
    D. there are no other tests available for isolating other pathogens from water

14. Sodium thiosulfate is added to bottles used for collecting water samples from swimming pools for bacteriological counts in order to

    A. facilitate subsequent plate counts
    B. neutralize residual chlorine
    C. reduce the turbidity of the water
    D. sterilize the bottles

15. The orthotolidine test used for determining residual chlorine in swimming pool water is a _____ test.

    A. bacteriological   B. colorimetric
    C. microscopic   D. precipitation

16. An operator of a swimming pool is ordinarily NOT required to test for

    A. bacterial count per ml of the water
    B. clearness of the water
    C. pH of the water
    D. residual chlorine

17. Imhoff tanks used for sewage disposal are PRIMARILY dependent upon the action of   17.____

    A. bacterial decomposition   B. chemical disinfectants
    C. high temperatures   D. water dilution

18. One of the purposes of a vent pipe used in connection with a plumbing system is to   18.____

    A. carry off discharge from wash basins
    B. carry off discharge from water closets
    C. protect trap seals
    D. provide a means of cleaning house drains

19. The term *cross connection,* as used in reference to plumbing systems, is to   19.____

    A. a connecting pipe which joins two other pipes of the same line
    B. a connection between a potable water line and a waste or sewer line
    C. the connection between a house drain and a house sewer
    D. the joining of waste pipes from several fixtures

20. Of the following, the one which is NOT used as a rodenticide is   20.____

    A. Antu   B. methoxychlor
    C. sodium fluoroacetate D. Warfarin

21. In rodent control, the PRIMARY method of producing permanent results is   21.____

    A. fumigating   B. poisoning
    C. proofing   D. trapping

22. The use of DDT insecticide as a residual spray is EFFECTIVE because it is a   22.____

    A. contact poison   B. fumigant
    C. respiratory poison D. stomach poison

23. The one of the following which is NOT used as an insect repellent is   23.____

    A. dimethyl phthalate   B. Indalone
    C. Rutgers 6-12   D. 1080

24. The one of the following which is ordinarily NOT used as a fumigant is   24.____

    A. ethylene oxide   B. hydrogen cyanide
    C. methyl bromide   D. phosphorus pentoxide

25. Certification of coal-tar hair dyes to be used in beauty parlors is made in accordance with the provisions of the   25.____

    A. Federal Food, Drug and Cosmetic Act
    B. Federal Labeling Act
    C. State Agriculture and Markets Law
    D. State Education Law

26. The unit used to express the MAXIMUM permissible weekly dose of ionizing radiation for human beings is the   26.____

    A. eV   B. MKS   C. MPN   D. REM

27. The half-life of a radioactive element is a measure of its

   A. atomic weight
   B. biological effect
   C. penetrating ability
   D. rate of decay

28. Alpha particles are considered to be the SAME as

   A. cathode rays
   B. heavy hydrogen nuclei
   C. helium nuclei
   D. x-rays

29. The formula, $E = mc^2$, is known as

   A. Einstein's Equation
   B. Newton's second law of motion
   C. Planck's Equation
   D. Raoult's Law

30. Of the following, the one generally NOT used for the detection of radioactivity is the

   A. geiger counter
   B. ionization chamber
   C. photographic film
   D. polarimeter

KEY (CORRECT ANSWERS)

1.	A	16.	A
2.	B	17.	A
3.	D	18.	C
4.	C	19.	B
5.	C	20.	B
6.	B	21.	C
7.	C	22.	A
8.	A	23.	D
9.	C	24.	D
10.	D	25.	A
11.	A	26.	D
12.	D	27.	D
13.	A	28.	C
14.	B	29.	A
15.	B	30.	D

EXAMINATION SECTION
TEST 1

DIRECTIONS: Each question or incomplete statement is followed by several suggested answers or completions. Select the one that BEST answers the question or completes the statement. *PRINT THE LETTER OF THE CORRECT ANSWER IN THE SPACE AT THE RIGHT.*

1. Assume that you have been assigned to inspect a building reported to be infested by rats and to prepare a written report thereon.
   Of the following items covered in the report, the LEAST important one is *probably* the

   A. fact that rats appear to be feeding on the garbage of a luncheonette which adjoins the building
   B. name and address of the building owner
   C. record of past violations by the owner
   D. statement made by tenants regarding the presence of rats

   1.____

2. After completing an inspection of a food manufacturing plant, you submit a report of your findings to your supervisor. A few days later, you receive a memorandum from your supervisor indicating that the head of the bureau found your report inadequate. You are to re-inspect the establishment immediately. Your supervisor's memorandum lists the areas which he feels your report did not cover adequately. You, however, are convinced that your report is adequate.
   The BEST course of action for you to take at this time is to

   A. refrain from re-inspecting the food establishment unless directed to do so personally by the head of the bureau
   B. re-inspect the premises, submit another report, and then discuss the matter with your supervisor
   C. telephone your supervisor and insist that the matter be fully discussed before you proceed further with a re-inspection
   D. write a letter to the head of the bureau explaining why you feel your report was adequate, and wait for a reply before you re-inspect

   2.____

3. Assume that you have a close relative who is engaged in the practice of accounting. Following your inspection of a restaurant which is not in violation of the health code, you inform the owner that your relative is an accountant. You hand the owner the accountant's business card and suggest that your relative be considered for any accounting work needed. The owner then tells you that he would like to have your relative take over his accounting work.
   Your action in securing the restaurant's accounting work for your relative is

   A. *improper;* you should have discussed the matter with the restaurant owner after your regular working hours
   B. *improper;* you should not have suggested your relative for the owner's accounting work
   C. *proper* as long as the owner remains in full compliance with the health code
   D. *proper* provided that your relative does not discuss the owner's business with you

   3.____

35

4. A tenant of an apartment house telephones the department of health to complain that no heat is being furnished to her apartment. The complaint is referred to you with instructions to make a field visit. When you arrive at the apartment house, the tenant partly opens her door but refuses to allow you to enter the apartment. You explain the situation to the tenant, but she persists in her refusal to allow you to enter the apartment.
The BEST thing for you to do in these circumstances is to

   A. notify the tenant that if she refuses you admittance to her apartment, you may be required to obtain a court order directing her to allow you to enter
   B. place the complaint in your pending file and return to the apartment the next time you are in the neighborhood
   C. prepare a report setting forth that the tenant refused to allow you to enter the apartment
   D. take a reading of the temperature in the hallway and then estimate the temperature in the apartment

5. In the course of your inspection of a luncheonette, you note a violation of a provision of the health code relating to the unsanitary condition of food containers. You point out the condition to the owner as you begin to prepare a notice of violation. The owner becomes very angry and declares that the food containers are clean. To illustrate his point, he shows the food containers to two patrons seated at the lunch counter. Both patrons declare that the food containers are clean and suggest that you not *pick* on the owner. The owner then tells you that if you make trouble for him, he will make trouble for you.
Of the following, the BEST course of action for you to take is to

   A. inform the owner that you will return at a later date to complete your notice of violation
   B. refrain from giving the owner a notice of violation since he has witnesses to support his position
   C. serve the owner with a notice of violation
   D. telephone your supervisor, tell him of the condition of the food containers, and ask him whether you should give the owner a notice of violation

6. A provision of the health code requires food handlers to take a course in food handling sanitation. Your supervisor requests that when you visit food establishments in your district, you remind them of the code requirement. Your supervisor stresses that your visit is to be an educational one and that you are not to emphasize the mandatory aspect of this provision. Later, you visit a restaurant owner in your district who expresses strong reservations as to the practicability of releasing food handlers to take such a course.
The one statement which you should NOT make to the owner under any circumstances is that if his food handlers take such a course,

   A. future violations of the health code by the owner will receive special treatment since he is cooperating with the department
   B. his profits may rise since patrons prefer to eat in a place where food sanitation standards are high
   C. the possibility of food poisoning with attendant possible economic loss to the owner will be decreased
   D. the requirement of the health code is mandatory in this respect and must be complied with

7. During your inspection of a multiple dwelling, you find a serious violation of a provision of the health code. The owner claims that at one time the particular provision in question was sensible, but circumstances have changed and the provision should now be repealed. After listening to the owner, you are convinced that the health code should be changed as indicated by the owner. The CORRECT course of action for you to take is to

   A. give the owner a notice of violation and refrain from making any report to your office concerning the provision in question
   B. give the owner a notice of violation and suggest to your superior that the provision be reviewed as to its continued usefulness
   C. refrain from giving the owner a notice of violation since the provision is obviously outdated
   D. refrain from giving the owner a notice of violation until the courts rule on the constitutionality of the provision

8. Assume that you are in the apartment of a tenant who has complained that the landlord is not furnishing sufficient heat. Your thermometer shows that the landlord is furnishing sufficient heat to comply with the pertinent provision of the health code. You so inform the tenant. The tenant excitedly declares that you are using a *fake* thermometer and that you may be on the landlord's *payroll*.
   Under these circumstances, you should state that

   A. if the tenant has any allegation to make concerning your inspection or character, she should contact your department
   B. if these, allegations are repeated, you will refer the tenant for psychiatric examination
   C. the allegations constitute defamation of the character of a public officer, and that you will so notify the police department
   D. you will ask the landlord to speak to the tenant to vouch for your honesty

9. You have been assigned to investigate a complaint with regard to a certain fruit and vegetable stand. Your investigation does not disclose any violation. Upon informing the owner of the stand of your findings, he offers you a bag of fruit as a gift. You decline it. He then offers to sell you the bag of fruit below the retail price - at cost to him. You SHOULD

   A. accept the offer, but refrain from visiting the establishment again
   B. accept the offer, provided you are satisfied that the fruit is being sold to you at cost
   C. decline the offer because it is not possible to calculate the wholesale cost of the fruit
   D. decline the offer since acceptance would be improper

10. The term *FT/SEC* is a unit of

    A. density   B. length   C. mass   D. speed

11. A container can hold 100 pounds of water or 70 pounds of an *unknown* liquid. The specific gravity of the *unknown* liquid is

    A. .30   B. .70   C. 1.0   D. 1.4

12. A *calorie* may be defined as the amount of heat required to raise one

    A. gram of water 1° C
    B. gram of water 1° F
    C. pound of water 1° C
    D. pound of water 1° F

13. The acidity of vinegar is due to the presence of _____ acid.

    A. acetic   B. carbonic   C. citric   D. hydrochloric

14. The cleansing action of a soap solution is due PRIMARILY to its

    A. acid reaction
    B. increased surface tension
    C. neutral reaction
    D. reduced surface tension

15. Titration refers to a process of

    A. determining the normality of an acid solution
    B. determining the refractive index of a crystal
    C. extracting oxygen from water
    D. measuring the quantity of salt present in a saline solution

16. Which one of the following types of compounds ALWAYS includes carbon, hydrogen, and oxygen?

    A. Carbohydrates   B. Carbonates
    C. Hydrates   D. Hydrocarbons

17. The formula for nitric acid is

    A. HNO_2 B. HNO_3 C. NO_2 D. N_2O

18. Gastric juice owes its acidity, *for the most part,* to the presence of _____ acid.

    A. carbonic   B. hydrochloric   C. nitric   D. sulfuric

19. Insulin is a type of

    A. enzyme   B. hormone   C. sugar   D. vitamin

20. The organ which prevents food from entering the windpipe during the act of swallowing is the

    A. epiglottis   B. larynx   C. pharynx   D. trachea

21. Casein is a type of

    A. carbohydrate   B. enzyme   C. fat   D. protein

22. The MAIN function of the kidneys is to remove wastes formed as a result of the oxidation of

    A. carbohydrates   B. fats   C. proteins   D. vitamins

23. Vitamin C is ALSO known as _____ acid.

    A. ascorbic   B. citric   C. glutamic   D. lactic

24. Light passes through the crystalline lens in the eye and focuses on the

    A. cornea   B. iris   C. pupil   D. retina

25. An electron weighs 25.____

   A. less than a neutron
   B. more than a neutron
   C. the same as a neutron
   D. the same as a proton

KEY (CORRECT ANSWERS)

1.	C	11.	B
2.	B	12.	A
3.	B	13.	A
4.	C	14.	D
5.	C	15.	A
6.	A	16.	A
7.	B	17.	B
8.	A	18.	B
9.	D	19.	B
10.	D	20.	A

21. D
22. C
23. A
24. D
25. A

TEST 2

DIRECTIONS: Each question or incomplete statement is followed by several suggested answers or completions. Select the one that BEST answers the question or completes the statement. *PRINT THE LETTER OF THE CORRECT ANSWER IN THE SPACE AT THE RIGHT.*

1. An electron has a _____ charge.

    A. negative   B. positive   C. variable   D. zero

2. Isotopes are atoms of elements which have _____ atomic weight(s).

    A. different atomic numbers and different
    B. different atomic numbers but the same
    C. the same atomic number and the same
    D. the same atomic number but different

3. In the Einstein equation $E = mc^2$, E, m, and c^2 stand for, respectively,

    A. electrons, molecules, and (centimeters)^2
    B. energy, mass, and (light velocity)^2
    C. energy, mass, and (radioactivity)^2
    D. energy, molecules, and (light velocity)^2

4. Photosynthesis entails the absorption of

    A. carbon dioxide and oxygen and release of water
    B. carbon dioxide and water and release of oxygen
    C. oxygen and release of carbon dioxide and water
    D. water and release of carbon dioxide and oxygen

5. Ordinary body temperature is approximately 37 on the _____ scale.

    A. absolute   B. A.P.I.   C. centigrade   D. Fahrenheit

6. Bacteria are _____ chlorphyll.

    A. multicellular organisms containing
    B. multicellular organisms that do not contain
    C. unicellular organisms containing
    D. unicellular organisms that do not contain

7. The immunity acquired as a result of an injection of tetanus antitoxin is termed _____ immunity.

    A. artificially acquired active
    B. artificially acquired passive
    C. naturally acquired active
    D. naturally acquired passive

8. A virus is the causative agent of

    A. diphtheria   B. smallpox   C. syphilis   D. tuberculosis

9. Typhus fever epidemics are caused by

   A. bacteria   B. rickettsiae   C. viruses   D. yeasts

10. The one of the following tests used to determine susceptibility to scarlet fever is the _____ test.

    A. Dick   B. Schick   C. Wasserman   D. Widal

11. Generally, the type of individual immunity to disease which is of the LONGEST duration is brought about by

    A. antibody production stimulated by killed microorganisms
    B. antibody production stimulated by live microorganisms
    C. transfer of antibodies during pregnancy from an immune mother to her unborn child by placental transfer
    D. transfer of antibodies from one adult to another

12. Diabetes is considered to be a(n) _____ disease.

    A. communicable   B. contagious
    C. noninfectious   D. infectious

13. The genus *Mycobacterium* contains a species responsible for

    A. diphtheria   B. gonorrhea
    C. tuberculosis   D. whooping cough

14. The pH of a neutral solution is

    A. 3   B. 5   C. 7   D. 9

15. Of the following, the pair that is NOT a set of equivalents is

    A. .014% .00014   B. 1/5% .002
    C. 1.5% 3/200   D. 115% .115

16. 10^{-2} is equal to

    A. 0.001   B. 0.01   C. 0.1   D. 100.0

17. $10^2 \times 10^3$ is equal to

    A. 10^5 B. 10^6 C. 100^5 D. 100^6

18. The length of two objects are in the ratio of 2:1. If each were 3 inches shorter, the ratio would be 3:1. The longer object is _____ inches.

    A. 8   B. 10   C. 12   D. 14

19. If the weight of water is 62.4 pounds per cubic foot, the weight of the water that fills a rectangular container 6 inches by 6 inches by 1 foot is _____ pounds.

    A. 7.8   B. 15.6   C. 31.2   D. 46.8

20. *Dry-ice* is solid

    A. ammonia   B. carbon dioxide
    C. freon   D. sulfur dioxide

21. The fat content of normal milk is *approximately* 21.____
    A. 1%   B. 4%   C. 10%   D. 16%

22. The one of the following acids GENERALLY responsible for the natural souring of milk is _____ acid. 22.____
    A. acetic   B. amino   C. citric   D. lactic

23. From a nutritional standpoint, milk is *deficient* in 23.____
    A. iron
    C. mineral salts
    B. lactose
    D. protein

24. The man who is USUALLY known as the father of chemotherapy is 24.____
    A. Paul Ehrlich
    C. Louis Pasteur
    B. Elie Metchnikoff
    D. John Tyndall

25. The success of this country in building the Panama Canal was due to the successful conquest of yellow fever. 25.____
    The man who directed the study which led to this conquest was
    A. Joseph Lister
    C. Theobold Smith
    B. Walter Reed
    D. William Welch

KEY (CORRECT ANSWERS)

1.	A	11.	B
2.	D	12.	C
3.	B	13.	C
4.	B	14.	C
5.	C	15.	D
6.	D	16.	B
7.	B	17.	A
8.	B	18.	C
9.	B	19.	B
10.	A	20.	B

21. B
22. D
23. A
24. A
25. B

TEST 3

DIRECTIONS: Each question or incomplete statement is followed by several suggested answers or completions. Select the one that BEST answers the question or completes the statement. *PRINT THE LETTER OF THE CORRECT ANSWER IN THE SPACE AT THE RIGHT.*

1. The *Babcock test* is used in milk analysis to determine _____ content.

   A. butterfat B. mineral C. protein D. vitamin

2. The phosphatase test is used to determine whether milk

   A. has an objectionable odor
   B. has been adequately pasteurized
   C. has been adulterated
   D. is too alkaline

3. A lactometer is used in milk inspection work to determine the

   A. acidity of milk
   B. color of milk
   C. percentage of milk solids
   D. specific gravity of milk

4. Milk samples collected at milk plants should be taken from milk cans, the contents of which have

   A. not been stirred so that sediment does not appear in the sample
   B. not been stirred so that the growth of bacteria which thrive on oxygen is not encouraged
   C. been stirred in order to obtain a representative sample
   D. been stirred so that the percentage of dissolved oxygen meets required standards

5. In the holding process, milk should be pasteurized for at least 30 minutes at a temperature of about

   A. 115° F B. 145° F C. 180° F D. 212° F

6. Undulant fever, which may be contracted from milk, is caused by an organism known as

   A. Bacillus subtilis
   B. Brucella abortus
   C. Staphylococcus aureus
   D. Streptococcus pyogenes

7. The presence of *milk stone* or *water stone* in dairy equipment is

   A. *desirable;* it indicates that dairy equipment is modern
   B. *desirable;* it indicates that milking machines have been sterilized
   C. *undesirable;* it will increase the bacterial count of milk that comes in contact with it
   D. *undesirable;* it will greatly increase the percentage of water in the final milk product

8. The type of dairy barn flooring which is LEAST desirable from a sanitarian's point of view is

   A. asphalt
   B. compressed cork and asphalt
   C. concrete
   D. wood

9. *Curds* and *whey* are substances encountered in the manufacture of cheese. Of the two substances, usually one

A. is made into cheese; the other is a by-product used to feed animals
B. is made into cheese; the other is made into butter
C. is made into hard cheese; the other is made into soft cheese
D. refers to bacteria-ripened cheese; the other refers to mold-ripened cheese

10. Botulism food poisoning in the United States is USUALLY caused by

    A. eating fish caught in polluted waters
    B. failure to wash raw fruit before eating
    C. improper home-canning of fruits and vegetables
    D. tapeworms found in beef or sheep

11. The growth of pathogenic bacteria in preserved dates and figs is *inhibited* because these foods have a high _____ content.

    A. acid   B. mineral   C. protein   D. sugar

12. In the heating of the following foods during canning, the one which generally requires the LOWEST temperature to prevent microbiological activity is

    A. fish   B. fruit   C. meat   D. milk

13. Food poisoning cases in the United States are USUALLY characterized by _____ followed by death.

    A. long periods of illness
    B. long periods of illness rarely
    C. short periods of illness
    D. short periods of illness rarely

14. In the United States, food poisoning due to eating mushrooms is LARGELY attributable to

    A. failure to cook mushrooms
    B. failure to wash mushrooms
    C. mushrooms which are blue in color
    D. mushrooms which have not been cultivated domestically

15. Of the following, the food whose flavor is NOT improved by the addition of monosodium glutamate is

    A. cooked vegetables   B. fruit juice
    C. meats   D. seafood and chowders

16. A NEW method of food preservation involves preservation by

    A. chemicals   B. drying   C. heat   D. radiation

17. In grading meat, the term *finish* refers to

    A. distribution of fat   B. muscle hardness
    C. presence of tapeworm   D. symmetry of the carcass

18. Of the following preservatives, the one which may NOT be legally used in the preservation of meat is 18.____

   A. benzoic acid
   B. salt
   C. sugar
   D. wood smoke

19. A vitamin known to be effective in the prevention of pellagra is 19.____

   A. ascorbic acid
   B. niacin
   C. riboflavin
   D. thiamin

20. Eggs are *candled* for the purpose of determining 20.____

   A. calcium content
   B. size of the egg
   C. the presence of blood spots
   D. weight of the egg

KEY (CORRECT ANSWERS)

1.	A		11.	D
2.	B		12.	B
3.	D		13.	D
4.	C		14.	D
5.	B		15.	B
6.	B		16.	D
7.	C		17.	A
8.	D		18.	A
9.	A		19.	B
10.	C		20.	C

TEST 4

DIRECTIONS: Each question or incomplete statement is followed by several suggested answers or completions. Select the one that BEST answers the question or completes the statement. *PRINT THE LETTER OF THE CORRECT ANSWER IN THE SPACE AT THE RIGHT.*

1. Foodstuffs such as cereal and flour do not readily spoil as a result of bacterial action because such foodstuffs usually have a low _____ content.   1.____

   A. acid   B. ash   C. sodium   D. water

2. The presence of bacteria responsible for typhoid fever in a public water supply is PROBABLY traceable to   2.____

   A. fecal contamination
   B. excessive water aeration
   C. pus from skin lesions
   D. rotting animal and fish remains

3. Objectionable tastes and odors in public water supplies are, in the great majority of cases, due to the presence of   3.____

   A. algae and protozoa   B. animal remains
   C. dissolved oxygen   D. yeasts and molds

4. Atmospheric pressure as indicated by the mercury barometer at sea level is GENERALLY about _____ inches.   4.____

   A. 10   B. 15   C. 30   D. 45

5. The CHIEF objective of a sewage treatment and disposal system is to   5.____

   A. alter sewage by chemical treatment so that it may be sold as commercial fertilizer
   B. convert liquid sludge so that it may be used as drinking water
   C. convert sewage into a form usable as land fill
   D. remove or decompose the organic matter

6. *Warfarin* is GENERALLY used in the control of   6.____

   A. ants   B. flies   C. lice   D. rats

7. The control of the common housefly has been regarded as important because houseflies   7.____

   A. are a great nuisance although they are not responsible for the transmission of diseases
   B. may transmit diseases by biting humans
   C. may transmit diseases by contaminating food with pathogenic organisms
   D. may transmit diseases by injecting pathogenic organisms into the bloodstream of animals which are later eaten by man

8. The term *Anopheles* refers to a type of   8.____

   A. ant   B. louse   C. mosquito   D. termite

9. Galvanized iron is made by coating iron with

   A. chromium B. lead C. tin D. zinc

10. The amount of oxygen in the air of a properly ventilated room, expressed as a percentage of volume, is APPROXIMATELY

    A. 5% B. 10% C. 15% D. 20%

11. Field control of hay fever generally depends upon the effective use of a(n)

    A. bacteriostatic agent
    B. fungicide
    C. insect spray
    D. weed killer

12. An orthotolidine testing set may be used to determine the presence of

    A. bacterial growth in milk cans and pails
    B. chlorine in wash and rinse waters
    C. DDT dust in foods such as flour and sugar
    D. organisms responsible for the spoilage of shucked oysters

13. The one of the following which is NOT a characteristic of carbon monoxide gas is that it

    A. causes nausea and vomiting
    B. has a strong irritating odor
    C. interferes with the oxygen-carrying power of the blood
    D. is a common constituent of manufactured gas

Question 14.

DIRECTIONS: Question 14 is based on the following statement.

The rise of science is the most important fact of modern life. No student should be permitted to complete his education without understanding it. From a scientific education, we may expect an understanding of science. From scientific investigation, we may expect scientific knowledge. We are confusing the issue and demanding what we have no right to ask if we seek to learn from science the goals of human life and of organized society.

14. The foregoing statement implies MOST NEARLY that

    A. in a democratic society, the student must determine whether to pursue a scientific education
    B. organized society must learn from science how to meet the needs of modern life
    C. science is of great value in molding the character and values of the student
    D. scientific education is likely to lead the student to acquire an understanding of scientific processes

Questions 15-16.

DIRECTIONS: Questions 15 and 16 are based on the following statement.

Since sewage is a variable mixture of substances from many sources, it is to be expected that its microbial flora will fluctuate both in types and numbers. Raw sewage may contain millions of bacteria per milliliter. Prominent among these are the coliforms. strepto-

cocci, anaerobic spore forming bacilli, the Proteus group, and other types which have their origin in the intestinal tract of man. Sewage is also a potential source of pathogenic intestinal organisms. The poliomyelitis virus has been demonstrated to occur in sewage; other viruses are readily isolated from the same source. Aside from the examination of sewage to demonstrate the presence of some specific microorganism for epidemiological purposes, bacteriological analysis provides little useful information because of the magnitude of variations known to occur with regard to both numbers and kinds.

15. According to the above passage, 15.____

   A. all sewage contains pathogenic organisms
   B. bacteriological analysis of sewage is routinely performed in order to determine the presence of coliform organisms
   C. microorganisms found in sewage vary from time to time
   D. poliomyelitis epidemics are due to viruses found in sewage

16. The title which would be MOST suitable for the above passage is: 16.____

   A. Disposal of Sewage by Bacteria
   B. Microbes and Sewage Treatment
   C. Microbiological Characteristics of Sewage
   D. Sewage Removal Processes

Questions 17-18.

DIRECTIONS: Questions 17 and 18 are based on the following statement.

Most cities carrying on public health work exercise varying degrees of inspection and control over their milk supplies. In some cases, it consists only of ordinances, with little or no attempt at enforcement. In other cases, good control is obtained through wise ordinances and an efficient inspecting force and laboratory. While inspection alone can do much toward controlling the quality and production of milk, there must also be frequent laboratory tests of the milk.

The bacterial count of the milk indicates the condition of the dairy and the methods of milk handling. The counts, therefore, are a check on the reports of the sanitarian. High bacterial counts of milk from a dairy reported by a sanitarian to be "good" may indicate difficulty not suspected by the sanitarian such as infected udders, inefficient sterilisation of utensils, or poor cooling.

17. According to the above passage, the MOST accurate of the following statements is: 17.____

   A. The bacterial count of milk will be low if milk-producing animals are free from disease.
   B. A high bacterial count of milk can be reduced by pasteurization.
   C. The bacterial count of milk can be controlled by the laboratory.
   D. The bacterial count of milk will be low if the conditions of milk production, processing and handling are good.

18. The following conclusion may be drawn from the above passage: 18.____
    A. Large centers of urban population usually exercise complete control over their milk supplies.
    B. Adequate legislation is an important adjunct of a milk supply control program.
    C. Most cities should request the assistance of other cities prior to instituting a milk supply control program.
    D. Wise laws establishing a milk supply control program obviate the need for the enforcement of such laws provided that good laboratory techniques are employed.

Question 19-20.

DIRECTIONS: Questions 19 and 20 are based upon the following excerpt from the health code.

Article 101 Shellfish and Fish
Section 101. 03 Shippers of shellfish; registration
  (a) No shellfish shall be shipped into the city unless the shipper of such shellfish is registered with the department.
  (b) Application for registration shall be made on a form furnished by the department.
  (c) The following shippers shall be eligible to apply for registration :
    1. A shipper of shellfish located in the state but outside the city who holds a shellfish shipper's permit issued by the state conservation department; or
    2. A shipper of shellfish located outside the state, or located in Canada, who holds a shellfish certificate of approval or a permit issued by the state or provincial agency having control of the shellfish industry of his state or province, which certificate of approval or permit appears on the current list of interstate shellfish shipper permits published by the United States Public Health Service.
  (d) The commissioner may refuse to accept the registration of any applicant whose past observance of the shellfish regulations is not satisfactory to the commissioner.
  (e) No applicant shall ship shellfish into the city unless he has been notified in writing by the department that his application for registration has been approved.
  (f) Every registration as a shipper of shellfish, unless sooner revoked, shall terminate on the expiration date of the registrant's state shellfish certificate or permit.

19. The above excerpt from the health code provides that 19.____
    A. permission to register may not be denied to a shellfish shipper meeting the standards of his own jurisdiction
    B. permission to register will not be denied unless the shipper's past observances of shellfish regulations has not been satisfactory to the U.S. Public Health Service
    C. the commissioner may suspend the regulations applicable to registration if requested to do so by the governmental agency having jurisdiction over the shellfish shipper
    D. an applicant for registration as a shellfish shipper may ship shellfish into the city when notified by the department in writing that his application has been approved

20. The above excerpt from the health code provides that
    A. applications for registration will not be granted to out-of-state shippers of shellfish who have already received permission to sell shellfish from another jurisdiction
    B. shippers of shellfish located outside of the city may not ship shellfish into the city unless the shellfish have passed inspection by the jurisdiction in which the shellfish shipper is located
    C. a shipper of shellfish located in Canada is eligible for registration provided that he holds a shellfish permit issued by the appropriate provincial agency and that such permit appears on the current list of shellfish shipper permits published by the U.S. Public Health Service
    D. a shipper of shellfish located in Canada whose shellfish permit has been revoked by the provincial agency may ship shellfish into the city until such time as he is notified in writing by the department that his shellfish registration has been revoked

KEY (CORRECT ANSWERS)

1.	D	11.	D
2.	A	12.	B
3.	A	13.	B
4.	C	14.	D
5.	D	15.	C
6.	D	16.	C
7.	C	17.	D
8.	C	18.	B
9.	D	19.	D
10.	D	20.	C

EXAMINATION SECTION
TEST 1

DIRECTIONS: Each question or incomplete statement is followed by several suggested answers or completions. Select the one that BEST answers the question or completes the statement. *PRINT THE LETTER OF THE CORRECT ANSWER IN THE SPACE AT THE RIGHT.*

1. The difference between the boiling point and the freezing point of water on the Fahrenheit scale is 1.____

    A. 0° B. 100° C. 112° D. 180°

2. All amino acids contain 2.____

    A. calcium and carbon
    B. hydrogen and nitrogen
    C. iron and oxygen
    D. manganese and phosphorus

3. Acids and bases combine to form compounds known as 3.____

    A. colloids B. salts C. solids D. solutions

4. $C_6H_{12}O_6$ represents the formula for a(n) 4.____

    A. protein B. salt C. sugar D. oil

5. The soil pH which is suitable for MOST garden crops varies between 5.____

    A. 2 and 5 B. 5 and 8 C. 8 and 11 D. 11 and 14

6. The farmer who plants peas, clover or alfalfa improves the soil PRIMARILY by increasing the available amount of 6.____

    A. carbon B. hydrogen C. nitrogen D. oxygen

7. Phenolphthalein is *generally* used as a(n) 7.____

    A. buffer
    B. drying agent
    C. emulsifying agent
    D. indicator

8. Of the following, the one classified as a compound is 8.____

    A. aluminum B. ammonia C. nitrogen D. sulfur

9. The process in which a liquid is vaporized and then condensed is called 9.____

    A. crystallization
    B. decantation
    C. distillation
    D. filtration

10. The formula *4-8-4* used in fertilizers refers to 10.____

    A. calcium, magnesium, and sulfur
    B. calcium, nitrogen, and phosphorus
    C. nitrogen, phosphorus, and potassium
    D. nitrogen, potassium, and sodium

11. The CHIEF source of fuel energy for the living cell are

   A. carbohydrates and fats
   B. carbohydrates and proteins
   C. fats and proteins
   D. water and carbohydrates

12. The structures of the human alimentary canal, in the order in which food passes through them, are as follows: first the mouth and throat, and then, IN ORDER, the

   A. esophagus, the small intestine, the large intestine, and the stomach
   B. esophagus, the stomach, the large intestine, and the small intestine
   C. esophagus, the stomach, the small intestine, and the large intestine
   D. stomach, the large intestine, the small intestine, and the esophagus

13. Pepsin is a stomach enzyme which

   A. changes fats to fatty acids
   B. converts starches to sugars
   C. curdles milk
   D. reduces proteins to peptides

14. The substance responsible for the clotting of human blood is known as

   A. fibrinogen   B. hemoglobin
   C. plasma   D. serum

15. Of the following statements regarding endocrine glands, the one which is NOT true is that

   A. endocrine glands have tubes or ducts to discharge their products to areas of use
   B. hormones are produced in endocrine glands
   C. the adrenal gland is an example of an endocrine gland
   D. the secretions of endocrine glands may be found in the bloodstream

16. The enzyme responsible for breaking fat and fat-like substances into glycerol and fatty acids is

   A. amylase   B. coagulase   C. lipase   D. oxidase

17. An acute x-ray dose of 600 roentgens applied to the entire body is

   A. insignificant except in the case of persons with an abnormally low level of tolerance to x-rays
   B. nearly always fatal
   C. severe in the view of some radiologists and should be avoided as a regular matter unless a person is employed as an x-ray technician
   D. tolerable in the average person, but such doses should not be applied more than once monthly

18. Radiations may cause cancer, yet radiations are used to treat cancer. This statement is

   A. *false;* radiations cannot cause cancer
   B. *false;* radiations cannot injure cancerous cells

C. *true;* radiations injure malignant cells but not healthy cells
D. *true;* radiations injure malignant cells without doing proportionate harm to non-malignant cells

19. The uranium-238 atom contains 92 protons and 146 neutrons. The number of electrons in the U-238 atom is

    A. 54   B. 92   C. 146   D. 238

20. The nucleus of the uranium-238 atom contains

    A. electrons and neutrons
    B. electrons and protons
    C. neutrons and protons
    D. neutrons only

21. Assume that a sample of radium with an atomic weight of 226 contains 250,000 atoms. Assume further that the half-life ($T_{1/2}$) of the radium is 1,600 years.
    This means MOST NEARLY that in

    A. 1,600 years 125,000 atoms of the radium sample will have decayed
    B. 1,600 years the portion of the sample which will have decayed can be expressed by the formula $T_{1/2} = 250,000/226$
    C. 3,200 years the portion of the sample which will have decayed can be expressed by the formula $T_{1/2} = 250,000/226$
    D. 3,200 years the radium sample will have decayed completely

22. The scientist who demonstrated that smallpox could be prevented by inoculating the skin of humans with material from cowpox lesions was

    A. Edward Jenner
    B. Robert Koch
    C. Joseph Meister
    D. Theodor Schwann

23. Staphylococci appear under microscopic examinations as

    A. four cells arranged as a square
    B. irregular clusters resembling bunches of grapes
    C. pairs of cells
    D. rows of cells, beadlike or chainlike

24. *Phenol coefficient* refers to a measure of the

    A. amount of phenol which may be added to food for use as a preservative
    B. effectiveness of a disinfectant in relation to phenol
    C. percentage of carbolic acid found in solutions containing phenol
    D. rapidity with which phenol destroys capsulated bacterial cells

25. The Schick test is used to determine susceptibility to

    A. diphtheria
    B. smallpox
    C. tetanus
    D. typhoid fever

26. Infectious hepatitis is a disease caused by

    A. bacteria
    B. protozoa
    C. rickettsiae
    D. viruses

27. *Phagocytes* are
    A. antigens which are used in the production of antibodies
    B. bacteria which destroy red blood cells
    C. cells in the human body which protect it from infection
    D. pathogens which may be present during coughing and sneezing

28. The Breed method is generally used in the bacteriological examination of
    A. meat B. milk C. soil D. water

29. The magnifying power of a microscope may be determined by
    A. adding the power of the objective to the power of the eyepiece
    B. dividing the power of the eyepiece into the power of the objective
    C. multiplying the power of the eyepiece by the power of the objective
    D. subtracting the power of the eyepiece from the power of the objective

30. The statement regarding viruses which is NOT true is that they
    A. are all parasites
    B. are responsible for poliomyelitis
    C. contain desoxyribonucleic acid
    D. grow in animals but not in plants

Questions 31-35.

DIRECTIONS: For each of Questions 31 through 35, select the letter preceding the word whose meaning is MOST NEARLY the same as that of the capitalized word.

31. NOXIOUS
    A. gaseous B. harmful C. soothing D. repulsive

32. PYOGENIC
    A. disease producing
    B. fever producing
    C. pus forming
    D. water forming

33. RENAL
    A. brain B. heart C. kidney D. stomach

34. ENDEMIC
    A. epidemic
    B. endermic
    C. endoblast
    D. peculiar to a particular people or locality, as a disease

35. MACULATION
    A. reticulation
    B. inoculation
    C. maturation
    D. defilement

KEY (CORRECT ANSWERS)

1. D
2. B
3. B
4. C
5. B

6. C
7. D
8. B
9. C
10. C

11. A
12. C
13. D
14. A
15. A

16. C
17. B
18. D
19. B
20. C

21. A
22. A
23. B
24. B
25. A

26. D
27. C
28. B
29. C
30. D

31. B
32. C
33. C
34. D
35. D

TEST 2

DIRECTIONS: Each question or incomplete statement is followed by several suggested answers or completions. Select the one that BEST answers the question or completes the statement. *PRINT THE LETTER OF THE CORRECT ANSWER IN THE SPACE AT THE RIGHT.*

1. The immunity found in individuals who have recovered from measles is termed _____ acquired _____ immunity.

    A. artificially; active
    B. artificially; passive
    C. naturally; active
    D. naturally; passive

2. Decomposition of fresh or cold storage meats can be detected BEST by

    A. noting absence of surface moisture
    B. noting presence of *off* odors
    C. noting warmth when touched
    D. observing discoloration

3. Bacterial control of shellfish and shellfish growing areas is being based increasingly in this country upon the density of the Escherichia coli organisms in the waters from which shellfish are collected.
   The BEST reason for this is that

    A. E. coli are virulent pathogens which produce serious diseases in man
    B. the density of E. coli in water is relatively easy to determine by shellfish fishermen
    C. the presence of E. coli is an indicator of the presence of human wastes in the water
    D. shellfish which ingest E. coli have objectionable odors which canning cannot remove

4. Proper cleaning of dairy utensils entails rinsing with

    A. cold or lukewarm water followed by scrubbing with a detergent solution
    B. cold or lukewarm water followed by scrubbing with hot soapy water
    C. hot water followed by scrubbing with a detergent solution
    D. hot water followed by scrubbing with hot soapy water

5. Of the following, the MOST accurate statement regarding the use of chlorine in the purification of public water supplies is:

    A. A small amount of residual chlorine in the water is desirable
    B. Chlorine will destroy most bacteria in the water with the exception of the coliform organisms
    C. The amount of chlorine added to water should be less than the *chlorine demand* of the water
    D. The use of chlorine in public water supplies should be resorted to only in cases of emergency

6. Pasteurization entails the heating of milk to AT LEAST _____ for _____ minutes.

    A. 143° F; 15   B. 143° F; 30   C. 161° F; 15   D. 161° F; 30

7. The pH value of water is of considerable significance when chlorinating swimming pools. The reason for this is that chlorine functions BEST as a bactericide when the pH value of the water is

   A. *high;* also, a high pH water value reduces or prevents eye smarting
   B. *high;* however, a high pH water value increases the possibility of eye smarting
   C. *low;* also, a low pH water value reduces or prevents eye smarting
   D. *low;* however, a low pH water value increases the possibility of eye smarting

8. A test commonly used for determining the presence of chlorine in water is the _____ test.

   A. orthotolidine   B. phosphatase
   C. TPI   D. Weil-Felix

9. The chemical which is added to water samples from chlorinated swimming pools to neutralize residual chlorine is sodium

   A. bromide   B. carbonate
   C. hydroxide   D. thiosulfate

10. Some years ago, the city experienced an outbreak of food poisoning from potato salad which was kept in an enameled utensil. The vinegar present in the potato salad dissolved a sufficient quantity of a certain substance found in the enamelware to cause poisoning. The name of the offending substance was

    A. antimony   B. arsenic   C. cyanide   D. zinc

11. The common housefly, Musca Domestica, is a(n)

    A. biting insect which does not transmit disease
    B. biting insect which may transmit disease
    C. insect which does not bite and does not transmit disease
    D. insect which does not bite but may transmit disease

12. The name of the substance which it has been suggested be added to *sleeping medicines* to induce vomiting in the event of an overdose is

    A. chlorpromazine   B. ipecac
    C. reserpine   D. seconal

13. The statement which BEST describes DDT is:
    DDT is

    A. a contact insect poison
    B. an instantaneous poison
    C. effective against all insects
    D. non-toxic to humans

14. The application of 10% DDT dust to rat runways and burrows is

    A. *advisable,* since it will serve as an effective rodenticide
    B. *advisable,* since it will serve to kill fleas which infest rats
    C. *inadvisable,* since DDT in such amounts stimulates rat growth
    D. *inadvisable,* since rats will be forced to use alternate runways and burrows making their elimination more difficult

15. Oligodynamic action refers to the

    A. ability of extremely small amounts of certain metals to exert a lethal effect upon bacteria
    B. change in levels of chlorine dilution brought about by evaporation
    C. discoloration of tiles in swimming pools due to the excessive mineral content of hard water
    D. removal of organic materials from water by means of sedimentation and filtration

16. The term *BOD,* as used in sewage disposal, refers MOST NEARLY to the

    A. consumption of oxygen by microorganisms engaged in the decomposition of organic material
    B. contamination of oysters and other shellfish by pathogenic bacteria making them unsafe for human consumption
    C. formation of finely suspended sewage material due to vigorous aeration by powerful pumps
    D. removal of suspended or floating objects from raw sewage by screening

Questions 17-22.

DIRECTIONS: Questions 17 through 22 are based on the Health Code.

17. Assume that the applicant for a Health Department permit is under 21 years of age. The statement which BEST applies to such applicant is:

    A. Age is not a factor in the issuance of permits
    B. The applicant may be issued a permit provided he is 18 years of age or over if the commissioner waives the age requirement
    C. The establishment of an age requirement for various permits is left solely to the discretion of the commissioner, who may fix any age requirement he deems appropriate
    D. Under no circumstances may a permit be issued to a person under 21 years of age

18. Assume that a person enters a neighborhood pharmacy and asks that a barbiturate be sold to him. He gives the attending pharmacist the name of his physician and states that he does not have the physician's written prescription for such barbiturate with him.
    In such a case, the pharmacist

    A. may dispense a small amount of the barbiturate without requiring a physician's prescription
    B. may dispense the barbiturate in any amount the pharmacist deems reasonable provided the person is either personally known to the pharmacist or presents proper identification
    C. may telephone the physician and accept the physician's oral prescription subject to the physician's later submission of a written prescription
    D. must insist that he be given the physician's written prescription before he dispenses a barbiturate in any quantity

19. A restaurant owner keeps and houses a cat in his restaurant in order to minimize the danger of rat infestation. He also permits patrons to bring their dogs into his restaurant. The CORRECT statement concerning these actions is that the Health Code _____ the owner to keep his cat on the premises _____ visiting the restaurant with their dogs.

   A. permits; and is silent with respect to patrons
   B. permits; but prohibits patrons from
   C. prohibits; and prohibits patrons from
   D. prohibits; but is silent with respect to patrons

20. The Health Code provides that utensils, such as knives, forks, spoons, cups, and saucers, used in the preparation and service of food are to be cleaned after each use. The Code provides that such cleaning shall consist of _____ cleaning(s) with a suitable detergent in clean hot water followed by _____ rinsing(s).

   A. *one*; *one*
   B. *one*; *two* successive
   C. *two* successive; *one*
   D. *two* successive; *two* successive

21. The owner of a meat market uses certain dyes which impart color to meat. The use of such coloring matter is

   A. absolutely prohibited
   B. permitted if the owner displays a sign which informs consumers that he uses coloring matter
   C. permitted only if the coloring matter is applied to ground beef and to no other meat
   D. prohibited unless such use complies with the provisions of the Federal Meat Inspection Act

22. Homogenized milk is milk which has been subjected to a treatment so that after 48 hours of quiescent storage the percent of butter fat in the upper one-tenth portion of a container will NOT exceed the percentage of butter fat in the remaining portion of the container by more than

   A. 5%   B. 10%   C. 15%   D. 20%

23. The Health Code names certain chemicals which, under stated circumstances, may be added to the drinking water supply within a building for anti-corrosion or anti-scaling purposes.
   Of the following chemicals, the one which is NOT specifically authorized for this purpose is

   A. calcium bicarbonate   B. calcium hydroxide
   C. sodium carbonate   D. sodium hydroxide

24. The Code provides that water in swimming pools must meet a certain standard of clarity. This standard is based on the

   A. addition of a chemical to the water which causes a color change if the water does not meet the prescribed standard
   B. measurement by the laboratory of the turbidity of a sample of pool water

C. use of a black disc, six inches in diameter
D. visual inspection by a sanitarian without the use of any aids or devices

Questions 25-27.

DIRECTIONS: Questions 25 through 27 are to be answered SOLELY on the basis of the following passage.

The first laws prohibiting tampering with foods and selling unwholesome provisions were enacted in ancient times. Early Mosaic and Egyptian laws governed the handling of meat. Greek and Roman laws attempted to prevent the watering of wine. In 200 B.C., India provided for the punishment of adulterators of grains and oils. In the same era, China had agents to prohibit the making of spurious articles and the defrauding of purchasers. Most of our food laws, however, came to us as a heritage from our European forebears.

In early times, foods were few and very simple, and trade existed mostly through barter. Such cheating as did occur was crude and easily detected by the prospective buyer. In the Middle Ages, traders and merchants began to specialize and united themselves into guilds. One of the earliest was called the Pepperers – the spice traders of the day. The Pepperers soon absorbed the grocers and in England got a charter from the king as the Grocer's Company. They set up an ethical code designed to protect the integrity and quality of the spices and other foods sold. Later they appointed a corps of food inspectors to test and certify the merchandise sold to and by the grocers. These men were the first public food inspectors of England.

Pepper is a good example of trade practices that brought about the need for the food inspectors. The demand for pepper was widespread. Its price was high; it was handled by various people during its long journey from the Spice Islands to the grocer's shelf. Each handler had opportunity to debase it; the grinders had the best chance since adulterants could not be detected by methods then available. Worthless barks and seeds, iron ore, charcoal, nutshells, and olive pits were ground along with the berries.

Bread was another food that offered temptation to unscrupulous persons. The most common cheating practice was short weighing but at times the flour used contained ground dried peas or beans.

25. Of the following, the MOST suitable title for the foregoing passage would be:

    A. Consumer Pressure and Pure Food Laws
    B. Practices Which Brought About the Need for Food Inspectors
    C. Substances Commonly Used as Pepper Adulterants
    D. The Role Played By Pepper as a Spice and as a Preservative

26. The statement BEST supported by the above passage is:

    A. Food inspectors employed by the Pepperers were responsible for detecting the presence of ground peas in flour
    B. The first guild to be formed in the Middle Ages was known as the Pepperers
    C. The Pepperers were chartered by the king and in accordance with his instructions set up an ethical code
    D. There were persons other than those who handled spices exclusively who became members of the Pepperers

27. The statement BEST supported by the above passage is:

    A. Early laws of England forbade the addition of adulterants to flour
    B. Egyptian laws of ancient times concerned themselves with meat handling

C. India provided for the punishment of persons adding ground berries and olive pits to spices
D. The Greeks and Romans succeeded in preventing the watering of wine

Questions 28-30.

DIRECTIONS: Questions 28 through 30 are to be answered SOLELY on the basis of the following passage.

Water can purify itself up to a point, by natural processes, but there is a limit to the pollution load that a stream can handle. Self-purification, a complicated process, is brought about by a combination of physical, chemical, and biological factors. The process is the same in all bodies of water, but its intensity is governed by varying environment conditions.

The time required for self-purification is governed by the degree of pollution and the character of the stream. In a large stream, many days of flow may be required for a partial purification. In clean, flowing streams, the water is usually saturated with dissolved purification. In clean, flowing streams, the water is usually saturated with dissolved oxygen, absorbed from the atmosphere and given off by green water plants. The solids of sewage and other wastes are dispersed when they enter the stream and eventually settle. Bacteria in the water and in the wastes themselves begin the process of breaking down the unstable wastes. The process uses up the dissolved oxygen in the water, upon which fish and other aquatic life also depend.

Streams offset the reduction of dissolved oxygen by absorbing it from the air and from oxygen-producing aquatic plants. This replenishment permits the bacteria to continue working on the wastes and the purification process to advance. Replenishment takes place rapidly in a swiftly flowing, turbulent stream because waves provide greater surface areas through which oxygen can be absorbed. Relatively motionless ponds or deep, sluggish streams require more time to renew depleted oxygen.

When large volumes of wastes are discharged into a stream, the water becomes murky. Sunlight no longer penetrates to the water plants, which normally contribute to the oxygen supply through photosynthesis, and the plants die. If the volume of pollution, in relation to the amount of water in the stream and the speed of flow, is so great that the bacteria use the oxygen more rapidly than re-aeration occurs, only putrifying types of bacteria can survive, and the natural process of self-purification is slowed. So the stream becomes foul smelling and looks greasy. Fish and other aquatic life disappear.

28. According to the above passage, if the proportion of wastes to stream water is very high, then the   28._____

   A. amount of dissolved oxygen in the stream increases
   B. death of all bacteria in wastes becomes a certainty
   C. stream will probably look greasy
   D. turbulence of the stream is increased

29. The one of the following which is NOT mentioned in the above passage as a factor in water self-purification is the   29._____

   A. ability of sunlight to penetrate water
   B. percentage of oxygen found in the air
   C. presence of bacteria in waste materials
   D. speed and turbulence of the stream

30. Of the following, the MOST suitable title for the above passage would be:

    A. Oxygen Requirements of Fish and Other Aquatic Life
    B. Streams as Carriers of Waste Materials
    C. The Function of Bacteria in the Disintegration of Wastes
    D. The Self-purification of Water

Questions 31-32.

DIRECTIONS: Questions 31 and 32 are to be answered SOLELY on the basis of the following passage.

Processing by quick freezing has expanded rapidly. The consumption of frozen fruits and vegetables (on a fresh-equivalent basis) was about 8 pounds per capita annually in the years immediately before the Second World War. It exceeded 200 pounds in 2008.

One example of this growth is frozen concentrated orange juice. From the beginning of commercial production in Florida during the 2005-2006 season, the pack of frozen concentrated orange juice has grown until it amounted to more than 320 million gallons in the 2008-2009 season. That is enough juice, when reconstituted, to supply every person in this country with about 160 average-size servings.

Another striking change in the pattern of food consumption is the sharp increase in consumption of broilers or fryers, young chickens of either sex, usually 8-10 weeks old, and weighing about three pounds.

The commercial production of broilers has increased more than 500 percent since 2006. The number produced exceeded 1.6 billion birds in 2008. On a per capita basis, broiler consumption was about 20 pounds annually (ready-to-cook equivalent basis). This is roughly one-fourth as much as per capita consumption of beef and nearly one-third as large as per capita consumption of pork. Consumption of broilers in the years just after the Second World War was less than one-tenth as large as the consumption of either beef or pork.

Among the factors responsible for this rapid growth are developments in breeding that led to faster gains in weight, lower prices in relation to other meat, and improvements in methods of preparing broilers for market. When broilers, like other poultry, were retailed in an uneviscerated form, dressed broilers could be held for only limited periods. Consequently, birds were shipped to market live, and dressing operations took place mostly in or near terminal markets - the centers of population.

Thus, it is that consumers benefit both from the variety of products available at all seasons of the year and from the many forms in which these products are sold.

31. According to the foregoing passage, the number of broilers produced in 2006 was MOST NEARLY

    A. 320,000,000   B. 1,200,000,000
    C. 4,000,000,000   D. 5,200,000,000

32. According to the above passage, the per capita annual consumption of frozen fruits and vegetables immediately following the end of World War II

    A. cannot be determined from the above passage
    B. was 16 percent of the per capita consumption of 2008
    C. was most nearly in excess of 200 pounds
    D. was most nearly 8 pounds

Questions 33-35.

DIRECTIONS: For each of Questions 33 through 35, select the letter preceding the word whose meaning is MOST NEARLY the same as that of the capitalized word.

33. AEROSOL, a _____ dispersed in a _____ 33.____

   A. gas; liquid
   B. liquid; gas
   C. liquid; solid
   D. solid; liquid

34. ETIOLOGY 34.____

   A. cause of a disease
   B. method of cure
   C. method of diagnosis
   D. study of insects

35. IN VITRO, in 35.____

   A. alkali
   B. the body
   C. the test tube
   D. vacuum

KEY (CORRECT ANSWERS)

1.	C	16.	A
2.	B	17.	B
3.	C	18.	C
4.	A	19.	D
5.	A	20.	B
6.	B	21.	D
7.	D	22.	B
8.	A	23.	A
9.	D	24.	C
10.	A	25.	B
11.	D	26.	D
12.	B	27.	B
13.	A	28.	C
14.	B	29.	B
15.	A	30.	D

31. B
32. A
33. B
34. A
35. C

EXAMINATION SECTION
TEST 1

DIRECTIONS: Each question or incomplete statement is followed by several suggested answers or completions. Select the one that BEST answers the question or completes the statement. *PRINT THE LETTER OF THE CORRECT ANSWER IN THE SPACE AT THE RIGHT.*

1. Which of the following materials used in collecting water samples is LEAST likely to contribute contaminants to the sample?

    A. Glass
    B. Teflon
    C. Polypropylene
    D. Stainless steel

2. A prepared reference sample, inserted into sample processing as close to the beginning as possible, is known as a(n) _____ sample.

    A. audit
    B. control
    C. continuous
    D. blank

3. Which type of sampling plan is based on the judgment of technical experts?

    A. Intuitive
    B. Statistical
    C. Isokinetic
    D. Spatial

4. Of the following, the type of *blank* NOT generally used in laboratory analysis is

    A. solvent   B. system   C. method   D. trip

5. An analyst should MOST strenuously avoid imposing turbulence on water samples that are being tested for

    A. dissolved solids
    B. biotic content
    C. dissolved gases
    D. suspended particulates

6. Which of the following is NOT a primary factor in determining the appropriate device to be used in collecting air samples?

    A. The amount of air to be moved
    B. Altitude of measurement
    C. Opposing vacuum forces
    D. Nature of substance to be analyzed

7. _____ meters is GENERALLY considered to be the shallowest depth in a standing body of water that will assure an analyst of the absence of chemical or thermal stratification.

    A. 3   B. 5   C. 10   D. 15

8. The FIRST collection of any material for analysis is known as _____ sampling.

    A. reference
    B. primary
    C. dip
    D. control

9. The collection technique ESPECIALLY appropriate for sampling rivers for chemical constituents is

    A. static grab
    B. point sampling
    C. spatial gradient
    D. stratified dip

10. To insure initial air flow through sampling and analyzing equipment, air pollutant samples should be collected

    A. on the upstream side of the air mover
    B. as close to the air mover as possible
    C. on the downstream side of the air mover
    D. as far from the air mover as possible

11. The MINIMUM number of samples to be collected from a water distribution system is determined by the

    A. population served by the system
    B. capacity of the system
    C. linear range of distribution
    D. peak rate of distribution

12. A substance that is being measured or sought in any sample of environmental or chemical matter is called a(n)

    A. control   B. reagent   C. solvent   D. analyte

13. The volume of air in a high-volume sample is measured in terms of

    A. cubic meters
    B. proportion of dissolved gases to ambient air
    C. time lapsed during collection
    D. rate of flow through the collection device

14. Which is the BEST season, in temperate regions, to collect samples from lakes in which waters are mixed enough to allow representative readings?

    A. Winter   B. Spring   C. Summer   D. Fall

15. The standard, generalized method for separating a pollutant for analysis from an air sample is to

    A. impose gravitational separators
    B. use liquid media
    C. exploit differences in related substances
    D. leave the substances together, but catalog them with separate data

16. The ONLY accurate way to measure the content of waste-water samples is through the analysis of

    A. specific point samples
    B. grab samples from areas that are well-mixed
    C. samples from both upstream and downstream sides of the dump
    D. composite samples that are proportioned according to flow patterns

17. A pool of two increments that is reduced or prepared as a subsample for analysis is called a

    A. spike   B. gross sample
    C. control sample   D. continuous sample

18. Of the following, the one which is NOT an advantage associated with the use of static sensors in the collection of air samples is   18.____

    A. no requisite human supervision
    B. low cost
    C. high-volume efficiency rate
    D. operation without reliance on electrical power

19. A substance that absorbs and separates a contaminant from the remainder of a sample is a   19.____

    A. reactant   B. reagent   C. spike   D. control

20. When wastewater samples are being collected in order to appraise plant performance, the recommended sampling pattern consists of   20.____

    A. grab samples from different points during peak flow
    B. grab samples at regular time intervals over a random six-hour period
    C. composite samples over a 24-hour weekday period
    D. daily composite samples over a random seven-day period

21. One DISADVANTAGE associated with the use of dustfall jars for the collection of air samples is   21.____

    A. dependence on supervision
    B. limited long-range collection
    C. expensive operation
    D. failure to measure smaller particles

22. The MOST effective method for removing potential contaminants from equipment used in sample collection is   22.____

    A. steam washing   B. repeated boiling
    C. inert disinfectants   D. detergent scrubbing

23. The term for a sample value that disagrees in magnitude with its neighboring samples is   23.____

    A. variance   B. spatial outlier
    C. spike   D. range

24. Which of the following is a method for measuring particulate pollution in air samples?   24.____

    A. Bubbling
    B. Adsorption
    C. Introduction of a reactant
    D. Inertial separation

25. Compounds whose presence obscures the measurement of a substance by introducing an unrelated analytical signal are referred to as   25.____

    A. interferences   B. controls
    C. toxics   D. blanks

KEY (CORRECT ANSWERS)

1. B
2. A
3. A
4. D
5. C

6. B
7. B
8. B
9. C
10. A

11. A
12. D
13. D
14. A
15. C

16. D
17. B
18. C
19. B
20. C

21. D
22. A
23. B
24. D
25. A

———

TEST 2

DIRECTIONS: Each question or incomplete statement is followed by several suggested answers or completions. Select the one that BEST answers the question or completes the statement. *PRINT THE LETTER OF THE CORRECT ANSWER IN THE SPACE AT THE RIGHT.*

1. To determine the maximum load for a given wastewater treatment unit, an analyst should use _____ samples _____ flow. 1._____

    A. grab; collected during peak
    B. integrated; proportioned to the average
    C. integrated; that reflect the range in
    D. integrated; collected during peak

2. The AVERAGE rate of flow, in cubic feet per minute, through a mechanical air sampler is 2._____

    A. 10-20   B. 40-60   C. 100-130   D. 180-200

3. The obtaining of a representative sample from a flowing stream that contains particulate matter is known as _____ sampling. 3._____

    A. stratified   B. intuitive
    C. isokinetic   D. suspended

4. Of the following situations, the one MOST appropriate for the use of mechanical air samplers is for measuring 4._____

    A. a high volume of particulate matter
    B. dissolved gas content
    C. a specific chemical substance
    D. and separating particulate matter by size

5. The CORRECT term for introduced samples in a procedure that do not contain the substance of interest, but are otherwise composed the same as actual samples, is 5._____

    A. controls   B. spikes   C. fields   D. blanks

6. The number of sampling replications required to sufficient-ly characterize a water body is decided PRIMARILY by the 6._____

    A. size of the water body
    B. stratification of the water body
    C. climatic conditions influencing the state of the water body
    D. purpose of the sampling

7. When sampling is done for the purpose of monitoring quality, sample replication can be expressed in terms of each of the following EXCEPT 7._____

    A. confidence limits   B. arithmetic means
    C. expanded controls   D. standard deviations

8. The MOST common method for measuring the amount of particulate matter in an air sample is

   A. weighing the sampler's filter before and after collection
   B. recording level of chemical activity with an introduced reactant
   C. determining volume ratios based on the rate of flow
   D. a strictly calibrated volume measurement

9. The use of single point samples in wastewater analysis is considered ACCEPTABLE in the determination of

   A. the capacity of the system
   B. specific chemical substance content
   C. representative waste flow during operation hours
   D. compliance with discharge regulations

10. Which of the following types of water bodies contains the HIGHEST variability of chemical constituents?

    A. Freshwater lakes
    B. Near-shore marine environments
    C. Deep, rapidly flowing streams
    D. Shallow, slowly flowing streams

11. The type of sample against which the results of a procedure are judged is known as a(n)

    A. blank   B. spike   C. control   D. analyte

12. The MOST common method for removing dissolved gases from a given air sample is through

    A. adsorption with solids
    B. absorption into a liquid medium
    C. inertial separation
    D. filtration

13. In collecting samples from relatively shallow, rapidly flowing streams and rivers, an analyst should be aware that such streams

    A. contain widely varying constituents at different depths
    B. cannot be representatively sampled
    C. are not consistently stratified
    D. can be sufficiently sampled at one point

14. In sampling wastewater, the term for the time period or volume of waste for which a composite estimate is desired is the

    A. spatial gradient   B. composite range
    C. minimum range   D. primary sampling unit

15. The type of introduced sample used PRIMARILY by analysts as tools for assessing and controlling sample contamination is

    A. blanks   B. interferences
    C. reagents   D. controls

16. Which sampling pattern is the MOST commonly used in the monitoring of sewer use?

    A. Long-term composite samples at a point far downstream from the discharge
    B. Grab samples from different critical points in the system
    C. Composite samples from a point as close to the primary discharge as possible
    D. Composite samples from different critical points in the system

17. The one of the following sampling/collecting materials MOST likely to contribute a chloroform contaminant to a water sample is

    A. fiberglas-reinforced epoxy (FRE)
    B. threaded PVC conduit
    C. polypropylene
    D. cemented PVC conduit

18. The MOST common motivation for sealing samples in their collection vessels is

    A. analysis of clear biotic potential
    B. prevention of dissolving particulate matter
    C. analysis of volatile compound content
    D. prevention of contamination from ambient air

19. If seasonal variations are of interest in a given water supply, monitoring samples should be collected

    A. hourly   B. daily   C. weekly   D. monthly

20. Which of the following types of *blanks* is NOT generally used in field collecting?

    A. Sampling media   B. Reagent
    C. Equipment   D. Matched-matrix

21. The collection medium for MOST high-volume air samplers is a

    A. borosilicate glass collection jar
    B. silica gel absorber
    C. glass fiber filter
    D. distilled, inert liquid

22. Of the following situations, the one which is MOST appropriate for the use of static sensors in the process of collection air samples is for

    A. collecting a specific volume of air
    B. separating sample content throughout time gradients
    C. measuring dissolved gases
    D. long-term collection of particulates

23. A deep, rapidly flowing river is _____ stratified _____ .

    A. usually; into fairly consistent thermal zones
    B. more likely to be; thermally than chemically
    C. more likely to be; than a standing body of water
    D. more likely to be; chemically than thermally

24. The type of sampling plan MOST likely to provide a basis for making probabilistic conclusions that are independent of personal judgment is

   A. statistical
   B. isokinetic
   C. primary
   D. intuitive

25. Generally, the BEST location from which to collect representative samples from smooth-flowing rivers that are above any tidal influences is at

   A. the surface
   B. near-shore eddies
   C. mid-depth
   D. lower depths

KEY (CORRECT ANSWERS)

1. D
2. B
3. C
4. A
5. D

6. D
7. C
8. A
9. D
10. B

11. C
12. B
13. C
14. D
15. A

16. D
17. B
18. C
19. C
20. B

21. C
22. D
23. D
24. A
25. C

EXAMINATION SECTION
TEST 1

DIRECTIONS: Each question or incomplete statement is followed by several suggested answers or completions. Select the one that BEST answers the question or completes the statement. *PRINT THE LETTER OF THE CORRECT ANSWER IN THE SPACE AT THE RIGHT.*

1. The MOST efficient devices to measure the gaseous pollutant content of an air sample are

    A. cyclones
    B. filters
    C. bubblers
    D. settling chambers

    1.____

2. The source MOST likely to cause high concentrations of toxic metals associated with nonpoint source water pollution is

    A. construction
    B. highway de-icing
    C. on-site sewage disposal
    D. urban storm runoff

    2.____

3. In the United States, the required landfill space per person each year is GENERALLY

    A. ten cubic feet
    B. one cubic yard
    C. one cubic acre
    D. ten square feet

    3.____

4. The easiest and most effective method for controlling air pollution is

    A. source correction
    B. treatment
    C. collection
    D. dispersion

    4.____

5. The MOST serious source of air pollution associated with the automobile is the

    A. fuel tank
    B. carburetor
    C. crankcase
    D. exhaust

    5.____

6. Which of the following practices or devices is considered to be a collection or treatment control for urban storm-water runoff?

    A. Anti-littering laws
    B. Street cleaning
    C. Floodplain zoning
    D. Detention systems

    6.____

7. The increasing trend in solid waste disposal in the United States is toward the practice of

    A. incineration
    B. ocean dumping
    C. sanitary landfill
    D. recycling/resource reclamation

    7.____

8. The MOST widely practiced method for cooling air pollutants before they reach control equipment is

    A. dilution
    B. settling
    C. heat exchange coils
    D. quenching

    8.____

9. Which of the following is NOT a factor of required knowledge for solving an upgrade problem in wastewater treatment plants?

    9.____

A. Staffing pattern
B. Normal operational and maintenance procedures
C. Daily peak flow rates
D. Condition of process hardware

10. The category of solid waste that constitutes the GREATEST volume percentage in the United States is

    A. residential
    B. bulky wastes
    C. commercial
    D. industrial

11. In current practice, the SIMPLEST test for ozone content of an air sample measures the air's reaction with

    A. metals with high lead content
    B. rubber
    C. organics
    D. copper

12. High concentrations of acid pollutants associated with nonpoint source water pollution are MOST likely to be contributed by

    A. non-coal mining
    B. air pollution fallout
    C. agriculture
    D. forestry

13. Which of the following methods is used by analysts to measure the concentration of hydrocarbons in an air supply?

    A. Chemical luminescence
    B. Flame ionization
    C. Infrared spectrometry
    D. High-volume sampling

14. Environmental engineers generally consider _____ to be the BEST cover material for sanitary landfill sites.

    A. sandy loam
    B. clay
    C. gravel
    D. silt

15. Deceleration of an automobile is most likely to cause the HIGHEST relative increase in the amount of

    A. hydrocarbons
    B. carbon monoxide
    C. nitrogen oxides
    D. lead

16. The _____ method for sanitary landfilling involves the distribution of waste into discrete *cells*.

    A. slope   B. area   C. ramp   D. trench

17. A DISADVANTAGE associated with the use of controlled burning for solid waste disposal is

    A. consumption of a large amount of resources
    B. lingering contamination of burn site
    C. increased transport costs
    D. large land area required

18. Each of the following is a primary factor in the determination of the area required for a sanitary landfill site EXCEPT

    A. percent reduction, by compaction, of on-site refuse volume
    B. amount of cover material required
    C. total projected amount of refuse to be delivered
    D. average density of refuse delivered to landfill

19. The method of solid waste disposal that currently involves the GREATEST costs in capital investment is

    A. incineration
    B. ocean dumping
    C. landfilling
    D. composting

20. The substance normally used in filters to detect the presence of sulfur dioxide in an air sample is

    A. microorganisms
    B. sulfur
    C. lead peroxide
    D. carbon

21. Which of the following is NOT a quality parameter of concern in the activated carbon treatment of wastewater?

    A. Heavy metals
    B. Suspended solids
    C. Trace organics
    D. Dissolved oxygen

22. The problem that presents the GREATEST potential hazard to landfill sites is

    A. pests
    B. water pollution
    C. gas
    D. decomposition

23. The MOST serious problem associated with the investigative practice of industrial stack sampling is

    A. control of potentially great capital expense
    B. risk of obtaining an unrepresentative sample
    C. safety risks for analysts
    D. skewing of sample readings by heat concentrations

24. The MOST common method for disinfection in wastewater treatment plants is

    A. ozone treatment
    B. ultraviolet light exposure
    C. chlorination
    D. introduction of bromine chloride

25. Of the following categories for the pollution control of urban stormwater runoff, _____ controls are considered to be the MOST effective and inexpensive.

    A. planning
    B. accumulation
    C. treatment
    D. collection

KEY (CORRECT ANSWERS)

1. C
2. D
3. B
4. A
5. D

6. D
7. D
8. C
9. C
10. D

11. B
12. A
13. B
14. A
15. A

16. B
17. C
18. C
19. D
20. C

21. A
22. B
23. B
24. C
25. A

TEST 2

DIRECTIONS: Each question or incomplete statement is followed by several suggested answers or completions. Select the one that BEST answers the question or completes the statement. *PRINT THE LETTER OF THE CORRECT ANSWER IN THE SPACE AT THE RIGHT.*

1. _____% of solid waste in the United States is considered compostible.

   A. 5-10 B. 20-30 C. 50-75 D. 80-85

2. Which of the following is NOT considered to be a factor affecting the level of organic decomposition in sanitary landfills?

   A. Moisture
   B. Surface area of fill
   C. Temperature
   D. Depth of fill

3. The SIMPLEST and MOST widely used device for controlling the particulate content of an air supply is the

   A. settling chamber
   B. adsorber
   C. wet collector
   D. bubbler

4. The agricultural practice MOST likely to contribute high levels of total dissolved solids to nonpoint source water pollution is

   A. animal production
   B. irrigated crop production
   C. pasturing and rangeland
   D. non-irrigated crop production

5. Pathogenic bacteria in wastewater supplies are likely to be produced by each of the following EXCEPT

   A. construction operations
   B. food processing industries
   C. pharmaceutical manufacturing
   D. tanneries

6. The substance MOST often used to remove sulfur from discharged flue gases is

   A. copper B. lime C. water D. acid

7. In controlling automotive emissions, an activated carbon canister is used to store emissions from the

   A. manifold
   B. fuel tank
   C. crankcase
   D. exhaust

8. Which of the following is NOT a disadvantage associated with the use of sanitary landfill sites for solid waste disposal?

   A. High collection costs
   B. Jurisdiction entanglements
   C. Large amount of land required
   D. Difficulties presented by seasonal changes

9. The Ringelmann scale is a device used to measure the _____ of an air sample.

   A. smoke density
   B. odor
   C. temperature
   D. gaseous pollutant content

10. High-volume sampling is a method for detecting

    A. ozone
    B. oxidant
    C. particulate
    D. sulfur dioxide

11. An example of air pollution abatement, as opposed to source control, is

    A. change of raw material
    B. modification of process
    C. equipment modifications
    D. stack dispersion

12. *Pollutant loading* is a term that defines the

    A. collection of pollutants for treatment in a control exercise
    B. quantity of pollution detached and transported into surface watercourses
    C. saturation point of any environment in terms of its pollutant capacity
    D. process of contamination, by an industrial source, of the ambient air

13. Each of the following is an advantage associated with the controlled burning of solid wastes EXCEPT

    A. land can be returned to immediate use
    B. sites are longer-lasting
    C. reduced amount of required land
    D. relatively easy collection and transport of materials

14. The device capable of removing the smallest particle from an air supply is the

    A. electrostatic precipitator
    B. settling chamber
    C. bag filter
    D. wet collector

15. High concentrations of suspended solids associated with nonpoint source water pollution are MOST likely contributed by

    A. urban storm runoff
    B. construction
    C. air pollution fallout
    D. non-irrigated crop production

16. Which of the following is NOT one of the primary steps involved in the control of gaseous air pollutants?

    A. Removal of pollutant from emissions
    B. Change in process producing pollutant
    C. Dispersion of the pollutant
    D. Chemical conversion of the pollutant

17. To control automotive air pollution, the process of recycling blow-by gases is a method for controlling emissions from the

    A. fuel tank
    B. exhaust
    C. carburetor
    D. crankcase

18. In testing a water supply for the presence of coliform bacteria, the survey method MOST likely to be used is

    A. oxygen demand
    B. dissolved oxygen
    C. total dissolved solids
    D. suspended solids

19. In measuring the constituency of a given air supply, analysts use the process of infrared spectrometry to determine concentrations of

    A. oxidants
    B. carbon monoxide
    C. sulfur dioxide
    D. particulates

20. Which of the following is NOT one of the primary factors affecting the choice of pollution control methods for urban stormwater runoff?

    A. Specific constituents of runoff
    B. Type of sewage system
    C. Status of area development
    D. Method of land use

21. A disadvantage associated with the use of sanitary landfill sites for solid waste disposal is

    A. high personnel and plant costs
    B. weakened accomodation of peak quantities
    C. potential for groundwater pollution
    D. difficulty with unusual, bulky materials

22. The MOST serious problem in air pollution is presented by

    A. cooling of pollutants
    B. treatment of pollutants
    C. collection of pollutants
    D. source modifications

23. Of the following practices or devices, the one considered to be an accumulation control for urban stormwater runoff is

    A. automobile inspection
    B. street cleaning
    C. floodplain zoning
    D. catch basins

24. _____ is used to survey an air sample for the presence of sulfur dioxide.

    A. Liquid medium
    B. Colorimetry
    C. High-volume sampling
    D. Flame ionization

25. Acceleration of an automobile is most likely to cause the HIGHEST relative increase in the amount of

    A. hydrocarbons
    B. carbon monoxide
    C. nitrogen oxides
    D. lead

KEY (CORRECT ANSWERS)

1. D
2. B
3. A
4. B
5. A

6. B
7. B
8. A
9. A
10. C

11. D
12. B
13. D
14. A
15. B

16. C
17. D
18. A
19. B
20. A

21. C
22. C
23. B
24. B
25. C

EXAMINATION SECTION
TEST 1

DIRECTIONS: Each question or incomplete statement is followed by several suggested answers or completions. Select the one that BEST answers the question or completes the statement. *PRINT THE LETTER OF THE CORRECT ANSWER IN THE SPACE AT THE RIGHT.*

1. Which of the following types of parameters is NOT generally considered to be one of the primary factors in defining environmental quality? 1.____

    A. Physical
    B. Meteorological
    C. Biological
    D. Chemical

2. All of the following resources are listed in the National Wildlife Federation's annual Environmental Quality Index EXCEPT 2.____

    A. timber
    B. human population
    C. minerals
    D. living space

3. In dollars, the costs of low air quality in the United States are GREATEST in relation to 3.____

    A. human health
    B. materials
    C. vegetation
    D. residential property

4. Evaluations of soil quality are MOST commonly expressed in terms of 4.____

    A. chemical contamination
    B. erodibility
    C. mineral constituency
    D. use of soluble nitrogen forms

5. Of the methods for water quality measurement below, which does NOT measure the effects of a given constituent? 5.____

    A. Threshold odor tests
    B. Bioassays of live fish
    C. Tests for chromium concentration
    D. Tests for *hardness*

6. Environmental quality indices are MOST successfully used for 6.____

    A. resource allocation
    B. public information
    C. scientific research
    D. enforcement of standards

7. In conducting water quality assessments intended to reveal the incidence of pathogens, _____ is MOST often the focus. 7.____

    A. nonpathogenic bacteria
    B. ammonia
    C. microscopic plants
    D. pathogens

8. Each of the following is a primary use of air quality data by state and local agencies EXCEPT 8.____

A. determination of compliance with standards
B. reporting daily quality levels to the public
C. determination of critical episodes requiring emer-gency measures
D. enacting quality legislation

9. Of the following units for evaluating the radioactivity of an environment, _____ is a measure of the activity of radioactive materials.

   A. rad
   B. dose equivalent
   C. curie
   D. roentgen

10. The one of the following that is NOT a factor in calculat-ing the average soil loss for a given crop rotation is

    A. temperature
    B. erosion control practice
    C. rainfall
    D. length of slope

11. Which of the following devices for assessing the quality of a radioactive environment offers the LEAST accurate quantitative measurements?

    A. Counter
    B. Ionization chamber
    C. Magnetic filter
    D. Photographic film

12. Solid-media water quality assessments that produce a green substance on the medium indicate

    A. algae
    B. coliform bacteria
    C. pathogens
    D. chlorine

13. The MOST important factor in determining the quality of a water resource is the

    A. purpose for which the water is being considered
    B. flow capacity of the resource
    C. chemical purity of the water
    D. biotic potential of the resource

14. According to the National Wildlife Federation's annual Environmental Quality Index, of the United States' resources, _____ is in the BEST relative condition.

    A. timber
    B. air
    C. water
    D. soil

15. Which of the following is NOT usually a component of quality of life surveys conducted in urban environments?

    A. Political
    B. Economic
    C. Ecological
    D. Health and education

16. Approximately _____% of the earth's water supply is drinkable.

    A. .5
    B. 1-3
    C. 3-5
    D. 5-10

17. A land-use quality index that measures the number of acres lost or gained to wildlife is known as a(n) _____ index.

    A. encroachment
    B. overlap
    C. habitat change
    D. urban green

18. Which of the following methods of water quality evaluation is considered a last resort by analysts?

    A. Measurement of factors associated with a given constituent
    B. Measuring the effects of constituents
    C. Qualitative descriptions
    D. Direct measurement of constituent concentrations

    18.____

19. _____ is NOT one of the primary impact standards by which air quality is evaluated.

    A. Esthetic   B. Meteorological
    C. Health   D. Economic

    19.____

20. The expression of pesticide injury to plants is a function of each of the following EXCEPT

    A. chemical properties of the pesticide
    B. sorptive ability of soil
    C. soil erodibility
    D. climatic conditions

    20.____

21. Of the following, experts have developed the LEAST definitive quality index so far for

    A. total environment   B. air
    C. solid waste   D. water

    21.____

22. Of the methods for water quality measurement below, which is an example of DIRECT measurement and reportage of a given concentration?

    A. Determination of the iron content of drinking water
    B. Determining water *hardness*
    C. Measuring alkalinity
    D. Turbidity analysis

    22.____

23. In order to determine the quality of a solid waste disposal management system, each of the following charac-teristics of solid waste must be measured EXCEPT

    A. particle size   B. density
    C. chemical makeup   D. waste source

    23.____

24. _____ is a measure of absorbed radiation dosage.

    A. Rad   B. Dose equivalent
    C. Roentgen   D. Curie

    24.____

25. According to the National Wildlife Federation, of the resources given below, _____ has the GREATEST relative importance to human life.

    A. air   B. wildlife   C. soil   D. water

    25.____

KEY (CORRECT ANSWERS)

1.	B	11.	D
2.	B	12.	B
3.	A	13.	A
4.	D	14.	D
5.	C	15.	C
6.	B	16.	A
7.	C	17.	C
8.	D	18.	C
9.	C	19.	B
10.	A	20.	C

21. A
22. A
23. D
24. A
25. C

———

TEST 2

DIRECTIONS: Each question or incomplete statement is followed by several suggested answers or completions. Select the one that BEST answers the question or completes the statement. *PRINT THE LETTER OF THE CORRECT ANSWER IN THE SPACE AT THE RIGHT.*

1. The appearance of a purple culture in the Gram-stain water quality assessment indicates a _____ result for _____. 1.____

    A. positive; microscopic plants
    B. negative; coliforms
    C. positive; blue-green algae
    D. negative; pathogens

2. The constituent LEAST likely to be measured by an Air Quality Index is 2.____

    A. hydrocarbon
    B. sulfur dioxide
    C. particulate
    D. carbon monoxide

3. A land-use quality index that is limited to assessing *man-made* environments is known as a(n) _____ index. 3.____

    A. encroachment
    B. overlap
    C. habitat change
    D. urban green

4. Which of the following is NOT an example of a quantitative water quality measurement based on an arbitrary scale? 4.____

    A. Suspended solids
    B. Volatile solids
    C. Acidity
    D. Color

5. The degree to which an environment can be considered *natural* is measured PRIMARILY in terms of 5.____

    A. the total species diversity of the environment
    B. the type of management imposed on the environment
    C. the degree to which ecological succession is allowed to take place
    D. its current station in the process of ecological succession

6. The ability of a soil resource to retain nitrogen is a function of each of the following EXCEPT 6.____

    A. altitude
    B. aeration
    C. soil texture
    D. temperature

7. The basis for judging whether a water resource is suitable for the uses under consideration is determined by 7.____

    A. absolute standards of purity and biotic potential that are established locally
    B. comparison of uses with projected capacity of the resource
    C. consensus of the population to be served by the resource
    D. comparison of data with published criteria concerning the purpose of the resource

8. For the sake of simplicity and comprehensiveness, MOST of the Environmental Protection Agency's quality reports take the form of 8.____

A. anecdotal reports B. bar graphs and charts
C. raw data D. time series plots

9. In measuring the ecological quality of an environment, which of the following categories of vegetation properties is NOT used as an indicator?

   A. Elemental composition B. Morphology
   C. Specific growth rates D. Species presence

10. Of the following devices for assessing the quality of a radioactive environment, the one designed to note the movement of single particles through a defined volume is

    A. photographic film B. ionization chamber
    C. magnetic filter D. counter

11. Of the methods for water quality measurement below, which is an example of a qualitative description?

    A. Microbiological content
    B. Floating matter and debris
    C. Turbidity
    D. Mercury concentration limits

12. According to the National Wildlife Federation's annual Environmental Quality Index, of the United States' resources, _____ is in the WORST relative condition.

    A. wildlife B. air C. water D. soil

13. Which of the following factors is NOT usually included in measurements of the effects of environmental noise on humans?

    A. Frequency spectrum
    B. Time variations of frequency and sound level
    C. Noise source
    D. Overall sound level

14. Most analysts agree that an accurate, readable index measuring the quality of a total environment would have to include _____ factors.

    A. fewer than thirty
    B. between forty and seventy
    C. no more than ten
    D. over 100

15. A soil quality index intended for measuring pesticide residue must be a function of each of the following variables EXCEPT

    A. irrigation practices B. pesticide
    C. crop D. climate

16. The method of water quality measurement considered by analysts to be the quickest and most accurate is

A. measurement of factors associated with a given constituent
B. qualitative descriptions
C. direct measurement of constituent concentrations
D. measurement of the effects of a given constituent

17. A land-use quality index that measures the proportion of developed to undeveloped land is known as a(n) _____ index.

    A. encroachment
    B. overlap
    C. habitat change
    D. urban green

18. Which of the following is NOT among the basic uses for environmental quality indices?

    A. Public information
    B. Ranking of industries by quality level
    C. Ranking of locations by quality level
    D. Trend analysis

19. The baseline alkalinity concentration criteria for a freshwater resource's ability to support aquatic life is generally considered to be _____ milligrams per liter.

    A. no more than 10
    B. between 5 and 50
    C. between 0 and 15
    D. no less than 20

20. In evaluating the quality of a soil resource, the MOST difficult aspect to determine accurately is

    A. aeration
    B. the form taken by nitrates
    C. moisture content
    D. total nitrogen content

21. All of the following are main classes of air quality measurements EXCEPT

    A. ambient air quality
    B. meteorological
    C. radiological
    D. emissions

22. _____ is MOST likely to cause taste and odor problems in a surface water supply.

    A. Coliform bacteria
    B. Fluoride
    C. Chlorine
    D. Algae

23. Of the methods for air quality measurement given below, which is used to detect and measure the incidence of carbon monoxide?

    A. Infrared spectrometry
    B. Chemical luminescence
    C. Flame ionization
    D. High-volume sampling

24. Of the methods for water quality measurement below, the one which is NOT an example of measuring factors associated with a given constituent is

    A. biochemical oxygen demand
    B. suspended solids measurement
    C. use of total organic carbon
    D. *indicator organism* tests

4 (#2)

25. According to the National Wildlife Federation, of the resources below, _____ has the LEAST relative importance to human life. 25._____

    A. air
    B. wildlife
    C. minerals
    D. living space

KEY (CORRECT ANSWERS)

1.	B	11.	B
2.	A	12.	B
3.	A	13.	C
4.	B	14.	D
5.	C	15.	A
6.	A	16.	A
7.	D	17.	D
8.	B	18.	B
9.	C	19.	D
10.	D	20.	B

21. C
22. D
23. A
24. B
25. B

EXAMINATION SECTION
TEST 1

DIRECTIONS: Each question or incomplete statement is followed by several suggested answers or completions. Select the one that BEST answers the question or completes the statement. *PRINT THE LETTER OF THE CORRECT ANSWER IN THE SPACE AT THE RIGHT.*

1. Which of the following devices is considered to be the MOST effective way of reporting a water supply's chemical composition data?

    A. table
    B. bar graph
    C. cross-referenced spread sheet
    D. circular graph

2. The type of data report which MUST be used as an integral part of any dataprocessing system associated with air quality measurement is

    A. data summarization
    B. diurnal variation pattern
    C. pollutant rose
    D. frequency distribution

3. The term for an analyst's attempt to detect and correct any errors that have entered the data set is data

    A. handling
    B. validation
    C. processing
    D. proofing

4. Of the types of data listed below, which one is NOT used as a parameter to define the physical characteristics of a lake?

    A. Surface area
    B. Average depth
    C. Underlying rock characteristics
    D. Retention time

5. The difference between the least and greatest values in a data set is known as the set's

    A. variance   B. range   C. mean deviation   D. mode

6. When experts in the same field disagree about conclusions drawn from a set of environmental impact assessment data, they sometimes privately answer a prepared questionnaire, and then distribute a summary sheet of opposing viewpoints amongst themselves. This method is known as

    A. the cooperative assessment model
    B. the Delphi technique
    C. the operational gaming model
    D. collective data validation

7. The term for calculated decrease In water pressure within a delivery system is

    A. vacuum   B. head loss   C. backup   D. flow gradient

8. Of the types of environmental impact data variables below, the one which is an example of an output variable is

    A. effects on natural and social environments
    B. population projections
    C. transportation networks
    D. economic growth

9. All of the following are factors required for the calculation of flow velocity in water delivery systems EXCEPT

   A. quantity of flow
   B. pipe material
   C. slope of hydraulic gradient
   D. temperature of flow

10. _____ errors in a data set are MOST easily estimated by the use of standard statistical techniques.

    A. Systematic   B. Random   C. Clerical   D. Standard

11. The one of the following which Is NOT an element of the data base needed in order to make decisions about water quality control is the

    A. physical characteristics of the water resource
    B. local needs and desires concerning use
    C. projected quality of untreated water
    D. present uses of resource

12. The air quality data report that consists of collected averages for a specific daily time period is the

    A. pollutant rose
    B. data summarization
    C. diurnal variation pattern
    D. frequency distribution

13. The concentration of bacteriological wastes in water is USUALLY expressed in terms of

    A. parts per million
    B. specific particle ratios, depending on the waste
    C. kiloPascals
    D. BOD

14. The one of the characteristics below that Is NOT used as a criterion for determining the quality of a data set is

    A. flexibility
    B. representativeness
    C. comparability
    D. completeness

15. In water delivery systems, water pressure is USUALLY measured in units called

    A. meters of head
    B. pounds per square inch
    C. flow gradients
    D. Pascals

16. In measuring air quality, extremes in data are often due to each of the following EXCEPT

    A. meteorological factors
    B. clerical misrecordings
    C. lab errors
    D. saturation of continuous data

17. The term for the difference between a data set's MEASURED and REFERENCED values is

    A. accuracy
    B. quantitative error
    C. reliability
    D. precision

18. In order to determine the storage needed to equalize a community's water supply demand at a constant pumping pressure, the MOST important data set needed is the

    A. exact pumping pressure
    B. time of daily peak use
    C. community's consumption rate
    D. delivery time between source and key use stations

19. _____ is the MOST commonly used method for determining the central value of a given data set.

    A. Mid-range
    B. Mode
    C. Arithmetic mean
    D. Median

20. What is the method for determining the standard deviation of values in a data set?

    A. Square root of the variance
    B. Half the total variance
    C. Average of all deviating values
    D. Average of the square roots of all deviating values

21. The MOST commonly used device for recording and reporting water delivery data at household sites is the

    A. compound meter
    B. digital register
    C. current meter
    D. disk meter

22. The term for the air quality data report that summarizes how often concentrations of specific magnitudes occur is

    A. frequency distribution
    B. data summarization
    C. pollutant rose
    D. diurnal variation pattern

23. Regarding environmental impact assessment, the goal of relating input and output variables in a data set is to

    A. validate the data set
    B. understand the consequences of imposing alternative policies
    C. establish a consensus about policy objectives
    D. compile an adequately useful data set

24. In order to calculate the intake capacity for a fire flow water delivery system, an analyst should compare the system's

    A. average pressure to the average distance of delivery
    B. total storage to the maximum amount of water needed
    C. maximum pressure to the maximum distance of delivery
    D. total storage to the average amount of water needed

25. Which of the distorting factors below is almost EXCLUSIVELY involved with the presentation of data, rather than the documentation?

    A. Mechanical error
    B. Bias
    C. Meteorological factors
    D. Clerical error

KEY (CORRECT ANSWERS)

1.	B	11.	C
2.	A	12.	C
3.	B	13.	D
4.	C	14.	A
5.	B	15.	A
6.	B	16.	D
7.	B	17.	A
8.	A	18.	C
9.	D	19.	C
10.	B	20.	A

21. D
22. A
23. B
24. B
25. B

TEST 2

DIRECTIONS: Each question or incomplete statement is followed by several suggested answers or completions. Select the one that BEST answers the question or completes the statement. *PRINT THE LETTER OF THE CORRECT ANSWER IN THE SPACE AT THE RIGHT.*

1. The determination of a drinking water supply's conformity with established bacteriological requirements is based on

   A. comparisons with dissolved solids data
   B. correlated oxygen content
   C. average measurement readings of all tests performed
   D. the number of positive tests

   1._____

2. The magnitude of error associated with a particular data set is known as

   A. systematic error
   B. data quality
   C. standard variance
   D. standard error

   2._____

3. Which type of air quality data report uses a circular figure for presentation, rather than a table or graph?

   A. Diurnal variation pattern
   B. Pollutant rose
   C. Frequency distribution
   D. Data summarization

   3._____

4. When the water pressure within a delivery system is greater than the atmospheric pressure, it is called

   A. gage pressure
   B. barometric pressure
   C. vacuum
   D. absolute pressure

   4._____

5. In data evaluation, the term for the variability of measurements of the same quantity gathered using the same method is

   A. standard deviation
   B. precision
   C. accuracy
   D. data variability

   5._____

6. The data used as the PRIMARY criterion for determining the amount of an allowable Industrial waste dump into a flowing stream is

   A. external climatic factors
   B. projected flow of the watercourse
   C. biotic potential of surrounding waters
   D. toxicity of waste material

   6._____

7. Once the data have been gathered for an environmental impact assessment, experts play a prominent role in each of the following ways, EXCEPT

   A. identifying alternatives and control variables
   B. relating input to output variables
   C. gathering more data using techniques of greater refinement
   D. evaluating reliability and applicability of data

   7._____

8. In determining the quality of a given water sample, concentrations of dissolved elements are expressed in terms of:

   A. volume
   B. mass
   C. particle ratios
   D. surface area

9. The errors in a data set that CANNOT be estimated by the use of standard statistical techniques, and usually produce a biased result, are called _____ errors.

   A. systematic
   B. random
   C. clerical
   D. standard

10. The method for data presentation MOST commonly used to illustrate the relationship between two sets of continuous data is the

    A. bar chart
    B. histogram
    C. block graph
    D. scatter diagram

11. _____ consumption is NOT part of the data set needed to quantitatively evaluate a community's water use.

    A. Average daily
    B. Peak hourly
    C. Peak daily
    D. Average hourly

12. The precision of a data set is BEST expressed in terms of

    A. mode
    B. standard deviation
    C. average
    D. frequency

13. In water delivery systems, the use of a manometer for measuring water pressure is

    A. usually limited to indoor, fixed units
    B. a universally adopted practice
    C. most commonly applied to mobile units
    D. seldom used indoors

14. All of the following are problems often associated with the practice of intermittently collecting air quality data EXCEPT

    A. inaccurate averages
    B. increased likelihood of extreme values
    C. greater meteorological impact on data
    D. increased susceptibility to error

15. Which of the following is NOT a method used to measure variation within a data set?

    A. Mean deviation
    B. Standard deviation
    C. Range
    D. Variance mode

16. The device MOST commonly used to report pipe flow data for a water delivery system is the

    A. table
    B. circular graph
    C. cross-referenced spread sheet
    D. nomograph

17. Of the following, the one which is NOT a problem often associated with using the operational gaming model for evaluating environmental impact assessment data is

    A. distancing of interested parties
    B. increased adventurousness of field experts
    C. introduction of human behavioral patterns into the assessment
    D. possibly inaccurate idealization of the system

17.____

18. The chemical analysis of a water sample can be used to determine each of the following factors EXCEPT

    A. dissolved solids   B. alkalinity
    C. biotic potential   D. pH

18.____

19. The air quality data report that groups data according to prevailing wind directions is the

    A. frequency distribution   B. pollutant rose
    C. diurnal variation pattern D. data summarization

19.____

20. The MOST commonly used device for measuring water pressure in delivery systems is the

    A. piezometer   B. Bourdon gauge
    C. manometer   D. barometric gauge

20.____

21. Each of the following is a problem associated with the use of existing data In making environmental impact assessments EXCEPT the

    A. possibility of different gathering techniques
    B. uncertainty of data accuracy due to time lapse
    C. unsuitabillty of data for an analyst's specific purpose
    D. personal bias of the analyst using the data

21.____

22. The data presentation method that works BEST for illustrating frequency distributions is the

    A. compass graph   B. table
    C. histogram   D. bar graph

22.____

23. The _____ is NOT a factor required in order to calculate storm runoff.

    A. maximum flow rate
    B. area's average rainfall intensity
    C. type and character of runoff surface
    D. minimum flow rate

23.____

24. Which of the characteristics of a data set is almost EXCLUSIVELY involved in the documentation of values, rather than the presentation?

    A. Accuracy   B. Representativeness
    C. Bias   D. Comparability

24.____

25. The MOST frequently appearing value in a data set is known as its

    A. variance standard   B. mode
    C. mid-range   D. median

25.____

KEY (CORRECT ANSWERS)

1.	D	11.	D
2.	B	12.	B
3.	B	13.	A
4.	A	14.	C
5.	B	15.	D
6.	B	16.	D
7.	C	17.	A
8.	B	18.	C
9.	A	19.	B
10.	D	20.	B

21. D
22. C
23. D
24. A
25. B

EXAMINATION SECTION
TEST 1

DIRECTIONS: Each question or incomplete statement is followed by several suggested answers or completions. Select the one that BEST answers the question or completes the statement. *PRINT THE LETTER OF THE CORRECT ANSWER IN THE SPACE AT THE RIGHT.*

1. Of the following, the LARGEST constituent component of average municipal solid waste (based on weight) is 1.____

    A. yard wastes
    B. glass and metal
    C. paper and cardboard
    D. miscellaneous

2. Of the following, which is a chemical element in municipal solid waste? 2.____

    A. Volatile matter
    B. Sulfur
    C. Paper and cardboard
    D. Water

3. Of the following, the component material in municipal solid waste which has an organic composition is 3.____

    A. aluminum
    B. pottery
    C. glass
    D. fixed carbon

4. Which of the following items is NOT included in the proximate analysis? 4.____

    A. Volatile matter
    B. Hydrogen
    C. Fixed carbon
    D. Moisture

5. _____ wastes are NOT a source of municipal solid waste. 5.____

    A. Industrial
    B. Household
    C. Commercial
    D. Institutional

6. The total amount of municipal solid waste delivered to municipal waste collection facilities is GENERALLY at a minimum during the 6.____

    A. spring   B. summer   C. fall   D. winter

7. The moisture content in municipal solid waste is HIGHEST 7.____

    A. just after a rain
    B. on Mondays because of weekend yard work
    C. after a holiday when there is no pickup
    D. all of the above

8. Until the recent initiatives for recycling, the average individual in industrial communities produced _____ municipal solid waste as/than those in rural areas. 8.____

    A. about the same
    B. more
    C. less
    D. it cannot be determined

9. The PRIMARY reason behind the increased public scrutiny about ash disposal practices is its concern about

   A. metals recycling
   B. heavy metals leaching into the groundwater
   C. jobs
   D. recycling everything

10. Under current Resource Conservation and Recovery Act requirements, in the design of sanitary landfills, it is NOT required to use a

    A. double liner
    B. leachate collection system
    C. leachate monitoring system
    D. methane gas powered electric generator system

11. Composting is an important factor for municipal waste collection unit operations because it

    A. removes materials from the waste which tend to burn poorly and increase nitrogen oxide emissions
    B. is the cheapest way to handle wastes
    C. makes a lot of money
    D. all of the above

12. The MOST important public relations characteristic of an operator is that he be

    A. trustworthy   B. a sharp looker
    C. college educated   D. a good speaker

13. The Clean Air Act

    A. allows the states to establish municipal waste collection regulations that are stricter than the federal standards
    B. prohibits the states from having municipal waste collection regulations that are stricter than the federal standard
    C. sets the maximum regulatory limit on municipal waste collection emission standards
    D. does not allow the consideration of economics in the setting of new source performance standards

14. In the _____, Congress authorized the Environmental Protection Agency to require the states to regulate existing municipal waste collection units.

    A. Standards of Performance for New Stationary Sources, Municipal Waste Collections
    B. Comprehensive Environmental Response Compensation and Liability Act
    C. Clean Air Act
    D. State Implementation Plan Act

15. The Clean Air Act requires each state to submit plans for implementing air pollution control and the Environmental Protection Agency to review and approve them.
    If this is not done, the state will be under threat of

A. losing their ability to regulate air pollutants
B. losing all federal highway funds
C. attracting less industry
D. all of the above

16. The Environmental Protection Agency New Source Performance Standard for new municipal waste collection units does NOT require regulation of

   A. carbon monoxide
   B. carbon dioxide
   C. nitric oxides
   D. dioxins and furans

17. The municipal solid waste characteristic that is UNACCEPTABLE at all municipal waste collection facilities is

   A. batteries
   B. medical waste discards
   C. tires
   D. radioactive wastes

18. Explosions at municipal waste collections can be caused by

   A. explosive munitions
   B. gas cylinders
   C. liquid drums of solvents
   D. all of the above

19. Of the following, the element of an integrated solid waste management system which can result in lowering the toxicity of manufactured materials is

   A. incineration
   B. recycling
   C. landfill
   D. source reduction

20. Of the following, the element of an integrated solid waste management system which will lower the metals and glass composition in municipal solid waste at the municipal waste collection is

   A. incineration
   B. recycling
   C. landfill
   D. source reduction

21. The element of an integrated solid waste management system which is generally considered to include composting is

   A. incineration
   B. recycling
   C. landfill
   D. source reduction

22. The recycling program activity which can reduce the potential quantity of formation of municipal waste collection acid gases is _____ removal.

   A. metal
   B. glass
   C. paper
   D. plastic

23. An average higher heating value of the municipal solid waste is APPROXIMATELY _____ Btu/lbm.

   A. 3,000
   B. 5,000
   C. 7,000
   D. 9,000

24. In general, the higher heating value of a large mass of municipal solid waste can vary from 2,000 Btu/lbm to maximum of about _____ Btu/lbm, depending upon how much mixing occurs and what is being charged.

   A. 3,000
   B. 8,000
   C. 25,000
   D. 50,000

25. The PRIMARY activity of a(n) _____ is to separate the light fluff fractions of municipal solid waste from the heavier non-combustible grit and glass.   25.____

    A. Trommel screen   B. shredder
    C. flail mill   D. air classifier

KEY (CORRECT ANSWERS)

1.	C	11.	A
2.	B	12.	A
3.	D	13.	A
4.	B	14.	C
5.	A	15.	D
6.	D	16.	B
7.	D	17.	A
8.	B	18.	D
9.	B	19.	D
10.	D	20.	B

    21. C
    22. D
    23. B
    24. B
    25. D

TEST 2

DIRECTIONS: Each question or incomplete statement is followed by several suggested answers or completions. Select the one that BEST answers the question or completes the statement. *PRINT THE LETTER OF THE CORRECT ANSWER IN THE SPACE AT THE RIGHT.*

1. The PRIMARY activity of a(n) _____ is to reduce the size of municipal solid waste pieces to around 2.5 inches across.

   A. Trommel screen
   B. shredder
   C. flail mill
   D. air classifier

   1.____

2. A population of 1,000,000 people on average produces about _____ tons of municipal solid waste per day.

   A. 350   B. 1,000   C. 1,700   D. 3,500

   2.____

3. The APPROXIMATE stoichiometric amount of air, in pounds, required to burn a pound of average municipal solid waste is

   A. 0.5   B. 3   C. 6   D. 15

   3.____

4. The typical amount of air supplied in a municipal waste collection unit for burning each pound of solid waste is about _____ pounds.

   A. 0.5   B. 3   C. 6   D. 12

   4.____

5. A refractory coating on the waterwall surfaces below the over fire air ports will

   A. reflect more of the radiant energy back to the combustion zone
   B. reduce the amount of heat extraction from the waterwalls
   C. cause higher combustion gas temperatures
   D. all of the above

   5.____

6. The air flow control device which provides the GREATEST precision of control on the air flow rate would be

   A. inlet vane dampers on a FD fan
   B. duct dampers
   C. variable speed driven motors on the fans
   D. all of the above

   6.____

7. A properly operating *in situ* monitor indicates 200 ppm of SO_2 in the flue gas when the moisture in the flue gas is known to be 15%.
   If an extractive instrument which has an in-line dryer indicates 235 ppm of SO_2, then the

   A. two instruments are reading consistently
   B. extractive instrument is reading too high
   C. extractive instrument is reading too low
   D. none of the above

   7.____

8. Properly operating extractive CEMS instruments indicate 200 ppm of SO_2 and 9% oxygen in the flue gas.
   The standard emission concentration of SO_2 corrected to 7% flue gas oxygen would be _____ ppm of SO_2.

   A. 200
   B. greater than 200
   C. less than 200
   D. none of the above

9. The uncontrolled particulate emissions in the flue gas (at the entrance to the APCD) from modular, starved air incinerators is about _____ that of conventional grate firing, mass burn systems.

   A. half
   B. twice
   C. ten times
   D. one-tenth

10. The overall amount of excess air used in refuse derived fuel fired municipal waste collections is about _____ that of conventional grate firing, mass burn systems.

    A. the same as
    B. 25 percent more than
    C. 25 percent less than
    D. twice as much as

11. The New Source Performance Standard for new municipal waste collections sets an upper limit on the temperature of the flue gas entering the air pollution control device. The limit was established to

    A. assure that there would be no condensation of flue gas in the APCD
    B. minimize formation of dioxin/furan compounds
    C. maximize the APCD particulate collection efficiency
    D. assure that there would not be any fires in the ESP or baghouse

12. Mercury emissions are a particular problem for combustion systems such as municipal waste collections because

    A. the municipal waste collection combustion environment provides unique conditions for vaporizing mercury
    B. mercury has a very high vapor pressure, even at relatively low temperatures
    C. mercury causes ash particulates to become sticky
    D. mercury substantially increases the weight of municipal waste collection ash

13. Which of the following statements about NO_x emissions from municipal waste collection systems is NOT correct?

    A. The temperature levels are too low to cause significant levels of thermal NO_x formation.
    B. The majority of the NOx is emitted as NO_2.
    C. The dominant source of NO_x formation is oxidation of nitrogen in the fuel.
    D. Flue gas recirculation will not be an effective NO_x control technique for municipal waste collections.

14. Carbon monoxide emission concentration is an indication to the operator and regulator of the

    A. overall combustion efficiency in the boiler
    B. color of the plume

C. temperature on the grate
D. quality of the bottom ash

15. A main concern about municipal waste collections which led to the development of new air emissions standards was the release of dioxin/furan emissions. Since these pollutants are toxic compounds, the Environmental Protection Agency had congressional authority to regulate municipal waste collection emissions by establishing a national emission standard for hazardous air pollutant (NESHAP).
If the Environmental Protection Agency had used that authority, which of the following statements would be TRUE?

    A. Regulations could be applied only to new units.
    B. Economic impact would be a consideration in setting the emission limits.
    C. The same emission limits would apply to both new and existing municipal waste collections.
    D. Different emission limits could be established for different classes of municipal waste collections.

15.____

16. In any combustion system, a portion of the inorganic material in the flue will be released as fly ash. For a pulverized coal fired utility boiler, about 80% of the ash leaves the boiler as fly ash.
The percentage of the fuel ash which leaves a refuse derived fuel facility as fly ash is APPROXIMATELY _____ %.

    A. 60-80   B. 40-60   C. 20-40   D. 10-20

16.____

17. In any combustion system, a portion of the inorganic material in the flue will be released as fly ash. For a pulverized coal fired utility boiler, about 80% of the ash leaves the boiler as fly ash. The percentage of the fuel ash which leaves a modular starved air facility as fly ash is APPROXIMATELY _____ %.

    A. 40-60
    C. 10-20
    B. 20-40
    D. less than 5

17.____

18. Refuse derived fuel systems use travelling grates because

    A. refuse derived fuel pieces are so small that they would jam up the air passageways if burned on pusher grates
    B. refuse derived fuel requires a thin fuel bed to prevent particulate entrainment
    C. since about half the refuse derived fuel burns in suspension, the refuse derived fuel on the grate does not clump up and need the physical bed mixing to provide air
    D. refuse derived fuel has more aluminum and glass than mass burned municipal solid waste, which makes clinkering on the fuel bed a more serious problem

18.____

19. When underfire air blows through the bed of municipal solid waste on a grate or hearth, the burning process GENERALLY proceeds

    A. from the hearth up
    B. from the top surface down toward the grate
    C. as a uniformly distributed flame condition throughout the entire bed
    D. according to the composition of the municipal solid waste

19.____

20. The combustion efficiency of a modern, water-wall municipal waste collection unit based on the overall utilization of carbon is

    A. about 25-40%
    B. about 70-85%
    C. about 85-95%
    D. greater than 95%

21. The combustion efficiency of a modern, water-wall municipal waste collection unit based on fuel energy to steam production is

    A. about 25-40%
    B. about 70-85%
    C. about 90-99%
    D. greater than 99%

22. Designers of municipal waste collections generally limit the steam temperatures to around 800F and the pressure to around 800 psia because

    A. unit efficiency is greater at high pressures and temperatures
    B. to go to higher temperatures and pressures would increase the cost of the pumps
    C. of concern about chloride corrosion in the superheater
    D. it is easier to maintain temperature and pressures at these values

23. Soot blowing is accomplished on a routine basis to

    A. keep a proper cake loading on the air pollution control devices
    B. blow off slag from the furnace walls
    C. to remove ash build-up from the tube surfaces in the convection section
    D. discharge excess steam produced in the boiler

24. Which of the following is an example of a negative pressure facemask?

    A. Constant supply of air is directed into the mask.
    B. Upon inhaling, air is drawn in through regulator or filters.
    C. Air passes from the inside of the mask to the outside.
    D. All of the above

25. A turbine/generator is running on load control. A sudden increase in load will cause _____ in the boiler steam drums.

    A. shrinking
    B. swelling
    C. foaming
    D. thermal stress

KEY (CORRECT ANSWERS)

1. B
2. C
3. B
4. C
5. D

6. C
7. A
8. B
9. D
10. C

11. B
12. B
13. B
14. A
15. C

16. D
17. D
18. C
19. B
20. D

21. B
22. C
23. C
24. B
25. B

———

EXAMINATION SECTION
TEST 1

DIRECTIONS: Each question or incomplete statement is followed by several suggested answers or completions. Select the one that BEST answers the question or completes the statement. *PRINT THE LETTER OF THE CORRECT ANSWER IN THE SPACE AT THE RIGHT.*

1. Employer compliance with OSH Act involves

    A. control of health exposures
    B. analysis of occupational safety and health statistics
    C. enforcement of employee obligations
    D. promulgating safety and health standards
    E. all of the above

2. What duties are triggered when the action level is reached?
    I. Exposure measurement
    II. Engineering controls
    III. Medical surveillance
    IV. Employee training
    V. Work practice controls

    The CORRECT answer is:

    A. I, II, III
    B. I, III, IV
    C. I, IV, V
    D. II, III, IV
    E. II, III, V

3. A serious penalty may be adjusted downward by as much as ____ percent.

    A. 40   B. 50   C. 25   D. 5   E. 10

4. The Federal Mine Safety and Health Amendment Act of 1977 transfers authority, for enforcement of mining safety and health, to the

    A. Department of the Interior
    B. Department of Labor
    C. Department of Health, Education and Welfare
    D. Bureau of Mines
    E. National Institute of Health

5. Safety and health regulations and standards which have the force and effect of law are issued by the

    A. Bureau of Labor Standards
    B. Occupational Safety and Health Administration
    C. Secretary of Health, Education and Welfare
    D. Secretary of Labor
    E. Assistant Secretary for Occupational Safety and Health

6. Court authority is necessary to enforce OSH Act to
   I. inspect when no advance notice has been given
   II. inspect records of industrial injuries and illnesses
   III. invoke criminal penalties
   IV. shut down an operation
   V. appeal OSHA actions

   The CORRECT answer is:

   A. I, II, III
   B. I, III, IV
   C. II, III, IV
   D. III, IV
   E. none of the above

7. A "serious violation" is defined as a condition

   A. where there is reasonable certainty that a hazard exists that can be expected to cause death or serious physical harm
   B. that has no direct or immediate relationship to job safety or health
   C. where there is a substantial probability that death or serious physical harm could result
   D. which is responsible for a fatality or multiple hospitalization incidents
   E. where a hazard is the result of unsafe work practices

8. The ____ is authorized by The Toxic Substance Control Act to require and obtain industry-developed data on the production, use and health effects of chemical substances and mixtures.

   A. Public Health Service Administration
   B. Occupational Safety and Health Administration
   C. National Center for Toxicological Research
   D. Environmental Protection Agency
   E. National Institute of Occupational Safety and Health

9. The Toxic Substances Control Act may LOWER the need for regulation by

   A. identifying hazards at the premarketing stage
   B. making OSHA more effective
   C. guarding against interagency duplication
   D. expanding research activities
   E. not issuing detailed workplace standards

10. How many other violations (exclusive of serious violations) that have a direct relationship to job safety and health and probably would not cause death or serious physical harm, must be found before any penalty can be imposed?

    A. 3   B. 1   C. 5   D. 10   E. 20

11. The ____ is(are) responsible for coordinating the technical aspects of the health program within the region.

    A. regional compliance officers
    B. area industrial hygienist
    C. area director
    D. national OSHA office
    E. regional office industrial hygienist

12. Horizontal Standards apply to

    A. establishing standards for engineering details
    B. all workplaces and relates to broad areas
    C. specific industries
    D. specific categories of workers
    E. establishing health and safety objectives

13. The ____ licenses and regulates the use of nuclear energy to protect public health and safety and the environment.

    A. Atomic Energy Commission
    B. National Institute for Occupational Safety and Health
    C. Radiological Assistance Program
    D. Bureau of Radiological Health
    E. Nuclear Regulatory Commission

14. Reviews of decisions of contested OSHA citations are conducted by the

    A. Occupational Safety and Health Review Commission
    B. U.S. Department of Labor
    C. Office of the Area Director
    D. State Supreme Court
    E. U.S. Court of Appeals

15. The compliance officer

    A. collects health hazard information
    B. shuts down operations where conditions of "imminent danger" exist
    C. collects appropriate samples
    D. investigates health complaints
    E. conducts an industrial hygiene inspection

16. OSHA defines "action level" as

    A. parity with the permissible exposure level
    B. concentrations below maximum allowable concentrations
    C. concentrations below minimum allowable concentrations
    D. one-half the permissible exposure level
    E. a reference point for control purposes

17. Which provision of the standard are employers obligated to when no employee is exposed to airborne concentrations of a substance in excess of the action level?

    A. Special training for employees
    B. Obtaining medical history statements
    C. Measuring employee exposure
    D. All of the above
    E. None of the above

18. Which of the following has the HIGHEST priority on OSHA's schedule of inspections?

    A. Response to employee complaints
    B. Random inspections of "high hazard industries"

C. Response to community complaints
D. Response to multiple hospitalizations incidents
E. Response to reported conditions of "imminent danger"

19. A non-serious penalty has been adjusted from $1000.00 to $500.00. The LOWEST amount an employer may pay if the violation is corrected within the prescribed abatement period is

    A. $500   B. $375   C. $125   D. zero   E. $250

20. Chemicals that are exempt from premarket reporting are those
    I. produced in small quantities solely for research
    II. used for test marketing purposes
    III. determined not to present an unreasonable risk
    IV. intended for export only
    V. used exclusively for commercial purposes
    The CORRECT answer is:

    A. I, II, III
    B. I, III, IV
    C. I, III, IV, V
    D. II, III
    E. all of the above

21. The purpose of federal supervision of current state programs is to

    A. establish enforcement procedure
    B. determine excess exposures
    C. establish procedures for measuring exposure levels
    D. provide technical advice for sophisticated engineering systems
    E. achieve more uniform state inspection under federal standards

22. Which OSHA standard consists of TLVs?

    A. Performance
    B. Health
    C. Design
    D. Vertical
    E. Horizontal

23. How many federal working days of receipt of notice of the enforcement action does an employer have to contest an OSHA citation or penalty?

    A. 10   B. 15   C. 30   D. 45   E. 60

24. The PRINCIPAL federal agency engaged in research in the national effort to eliminate on-the-job hazards is the

    A. National Institute for Occupational Safety and Health
    B. Occupational Safety and Health Administration
    C. Environmental Protection Agency
    D. Food and Drug Administration
    E. Mine Safety and Health Administration

25. The area office updates the workplace inventory data

    A. semi-annually
    B. yearly
    C. every 2 years
    D. every 5 years
    E. following each inspection

KEY (CORRECT ANSWERS)

1. A
2. B
3. B
4. B
5. D

6. C
7. C
8. D
9. A
10. D

11. E
12. B
13. E
14. E
15. A

16. D
17. C
18. D
19. E
20. A

21. E
22. A
23. B
24. A
25. B

———

EXAMINATION SECTION
TEST 1

DIRECTIONS: Each question or incomplete statement is followed by several suggested answers or completions. Select the one that BEST answers the question or completes the statement. *PRINT THE LETTER OF THE CORRECT ANSWER IN THE SPACE AT THE RIGHT.*

1. _____ should only be used in processes that are well-enclosed and isolated.
   I. Acetaldehyde
   II. Butyllithium
   III. Carbon disulfide
   IV. Butyraldehyde
   V. Chlorine dioxide
   The CORRECT answer is:

   A. I, IV
   B. I, II, III
   C. II, IV, V
   D. I, II, IV
   E. I, IV, V

   1.____

2. In spite of the high inherent toxicity, there are few cases of industrial poisoning with

   A. toluidine
   B. indium
   C. barium
   D. cadmium
   E. bensidine

   2.____

3. _____ acetate represents NO health hazard either from inhalation of vapor or contact of liquid with skin or eyes.

   A. Methyl
   B. Ethyl
   C. N-Propyl
   D. Vinyl
   E. Isobutyl

   3.____

4. Dinitrochlorobenzene is a

   A. highly toxic substance producing acute poisoning by absorption
   B. suspected carcinogen
   C. powerful skin-sensitizing agent
   D. proven carcinogen
   E. systemic poison

   4.____

5. What makes ethylenimine especially hazardous?
   I. It causes confusion and changes in reflexes.
   II. It is difficult to predict individual reactions.
   III. It lacks warning properties.
   IV. The onset of symptoms are delayed.
   V. Initial exposures produce feelings of euphoria.
   The CORRECT answer is:

   A. I, II
   B. III, IV
   C. II, V
   D. II, III
   E. II, IV, V

   5.____

6. Which of the following halogenated hydrocarbons is the MOST toxic?

   A. Tetrachloroethylene
   B. Trichloroethylene
   C. Methylbromide
   D. Methyl chloroform
   E. Tetrachloroethane

   6.____

7. Iodine is *most likely* to cause

   A. pulmonary irritation
   B. eye irritation
   C. edema
   D. skin irritation
   E. stomach distress

8. Perchloromethyl mercaptan differs from the other mercaptans by its
   I. insolubility in water
   II. strong odor
   III. stronger irritant ability
   IV. color
   V. gaseous state

   The CORRECT answer is:

   A. I, III, IV
   B. II, III, V
   C. I, II, III
   D. II, III, IV, V
   E. III, IV, V

9. Lethal poisoning has resulted from exposure to methyl

   A. iodide
   B. ethyl ketone
   C. isobutyl
   D. mercaptan
   E. demeton

10. The BEST way to protect workers from nitrobenzene is to

    A. require a complete bath and change of clothing daily
    B. require an air-supplied respirator
    C. require neoprene gloves
    D. employ local exhaust ventilation
    E. stress good housekeeping

11. The MOST desirable first aid treatment when oxalic acid has been taken internally is to

    A. administer an emetic
    B. force quantities of water
    C. administer black coffee
    D. administer milk
    E. force large quantities of strongly brewed tea

12. What is the route of absorption of Phorate, the insecticide?

    A. Oral
    B. Respiratory
    C. Dermal
    D. All of the above
    E. None of the above

13. Which of the following insecticides is about half as toxic as pyrethrum?

    A. Parathion
    B. Ethion
    C. Chlordane
    D. Rotenone
    E. Aldrin

14. Vinyl _____ is regarded as a human carcinogen.

    A. toluene
    B. bromide
    C. propionate
    D. chloride
    E. acetate

15. The safety of _____ is MOST affected by good housekeeping practices.
    I. sodium fluoroacetate
    II. trifluoromonobromomethane
    III. methyl isocynate
    IV. dibutylphthalate
    V. methyl acetylene
    The CORRECT answer is:

    A. I, II, IV B. II, III, IV C. II, IV, V
    D. I, II, III E. I, III, V

16. Allyl alcohol is used as a(n)

    A. solvent B. antifreeze
    C. fungicide and herbicide D. fuel
    E. dye

17. Which of the following is used in the salt mixtures on streets and highways to lower freezing points?

    A. Calcium chloride B. Sodium chlorate
    C. Indium D. Dichlorobenzidine
    E. Ethyl silicate

18. Diethylamine is used MAINLY in the _____ industry.

    A. dye B. food processing
    C. cosmetic D. pharmaceutical
    E. automotive

19. As used in industry, halogenated hydrocarbons are

    A. suspected carcinogens B. potent anesthetics
    C. skin sensitizers D. cholinesterase inhibitors
    E. low risk asphyxiants

20. Methyl chloride is MOST widely used as a

    A. herbicide B. fumigant
    C. dry cleaning agent D. fire extinguishing agent
    E. refrigerant

21. Workers exposed to phosphorus should have periodic

    A. dental exams B. chest x-rays C. eye exams
    D. blood tests E. urine tests

22. _____ may result after inhalation of high concentrations of acetonitrile.

    A. Laryngeal spasms
    B. Severe conjunctival and nasopharyngeal irritation
    C. Chemical bronchitis
    D. Severe and fatal poisoning
    E. Dizziness

23. Chlorinated polyphenyls are often called

    A. arochlors B. amobams C. ethions
    D. lindanes E. carbamates

24. Industrial workers have developed antabuse effects while manufacturing and handling
    I.   furfural
    II. disulfuram
    III. methyl isobutylcarbinol
    IV. thiram
    V.   carbon disulfide
    The CORRECT answer is:

    A. I, II, V
    D. I, III, V
    B. II, IV
    E. II, III
    C. I, III

25. _____ is a foul-smelling gas used MAINLY for giving an odor to things in order to make them noticeable.

    A. Isopropylamine
    C. Fluorine
    E. Ethyl mercaptan
    B. Sulfur pentafluoride
    D. Toluene

KEY (CORRECT ANSWERS)

1. B
2. C
3. D
4. C
5. B

6. E
7. D
8. A
9. A
10. A

11. A
12. D
13. D
14. D
15. C

16. C
17. A
18. A
19. B
20. E

21. A
22. D
23. A
24. B
25. E

TEST 2

DIRECTIONS: Each question or incomplete statement is followed by several suggested answers or completions. Select the one that BEST answers the question or completes the statement. *PRINT THE LETTER OF THE CORRECT ANSWER IN THE SPACE AT THE RIGHT.*

1. The 100 ppm TLV for hexane is to provide freedom from

    A. lung damage
    B. central nervous system effects
    C. damage to blood-forming organs
    D. fire and explosion
    E. skin burns

    1.____

2. Isophorone is classified as a

    A. powerful oxidizing agent
    B. primary skin irritant
    C. powerful methemoglobin former
    D. blood and nervous system poison
    E. human carcinogen

    2.____

3. Methanol poisoning has an exceptionally severe action on the

    A. digestive system mucous membranes
    B. central nervous system
    C. liver
    D. kidneys
    E. optic nerve

    3.____

4. The TLV for naphthalene may NOT prevent blood changes in

    A. anemic individuals
    C. pregnant women
    E. individuals who smoke
    B. alcohol abusers
    D. hyper susceptible individuals

    4.____

5. Nitropropane is CHIEFLY used as a

    A. nematocide
    C. fuel
    E. lacquer and dope solvent
    B. fumigant
    D. refrigerant

    5.____

6. Which of the following are symptoms of an oxygen-deficient atmosphere?
    I. Blue color of the skin and fingernails
    II. Headache
    III. Shivering
    IV. Eye sensitivity
    V. Respiratory congestion
    The CORRECT answer is:

    A. I, II
    D. II, III, IV
    B. II, IV, V
    E. None of the above
    C. I, II, III

    6.____

117

7. _____ MOST affects toxicity?

   A. Vapor pressure B. Flash point C. Boiling point
   D. Vapor volume   E. Specific gravity

8. Eye lesions caused by the dust of silver nitrate are FIRST seen in the

   A. sclera   B. caruncle C. iris
   D. conjunctiva E. cornea

9. Which of the following substances have a special warning for the prevention of cutaneous absorption so that the threshold limit is not invalidated?
   I. Trichloronaphthalene
   II. Trimethylbenzene
   III. Methyl isoamyl ketone
   IV. Sodium fluoroacetate
   V. Dieldrin
   The CORRECT answer is:

   A. I, IV, V   B. I, II, III   C. I, II, IV
   D. II, III, IV E. II, IV, V

10. Which of the following toxic substances has the LOWEST boiling point?

    A. Ethylamine   B. Dibutylphthalate
    C. Nitrotoluene   D. Isophorone diisocyanate
    E. Diglycidyl ether

11. Sodium chlorate is GENERALLY shipped in kegs lined with

    A. rubber   B. stainless steel
    C. glass   D. neoprene
    E. heavy brown paper

12. The toxicity of the chlorinated diphenyls is HIGHEST when the chlorine content is around

    A. 10% B. 1% C. 85% D. 50% E. 5%

13. Which of the following MOST resembles ammonia in its chemical and toxicological properties?

    A. Alpha-naphthylamine B. Triphenylamine
    C. Dimethylamine   D. Ethanolamine
    E. Aniline

14. Hydrazine, a rocket fuel, is capable of producing

    A. lung injury
    B. narcosis
    C. central nervous system depression
    D. severe skin burns
    E. acute poisoning

15. Amino benzene may be listed by the name

    A. aniline B. naphtha C. acrolein
    D. benzol   E. butanol

16. The LEAST irritating acid is 16._____

    A. nitric   B. phosphoric   C. sulfuric
    D. hydrochloric   E. hydrofluoric

17. The MOST common hazard associated with the wood-preserving industry is 17._____

    A. irritation of the eyes, nose, and throat
    B. dermatitis
    C. cumulative systemic toxic effects
    D. respiratory allergy
    E. chlorinesterase inhibition

18. Iodine must be used with caution because it 18._____

    A. is likely to cause skin irritation
    B. irritates the respiratory system
    C. is an anesthetic
    D. causes eye irritation
    E. causes structural changes in the cornea

19. The common name for phosphorodithiotic acid is 19._____

    A. amobam   B. thimet   C. phosdrin
    D. lindane   E. ethion

20. Which of the following conditions would preclude the individual from possible exposure to chloronaphthalene? 20._____
    I. Oily skin
    II. Dry skin
    III. Heart disease
    IV. Liver disease
    V. Kidney disease
    The CORRECT answer is:

    A. I, III   B. I, IV, V   C. II, III, IV
    D. III, IV, V   E. IV, V

21. Inhaled arsenic can be detected in 21._____

    A. fecal material   B. the blood
    C. saliva   D. urine
    E. all of the above

22. Which of the following liquids are non-flammable? 22._____
    I. Carbon disulfide
    II. Hydrogen peroxide
    III. Phosphorus trichloride
    IV. Chloroform
    V. Propylene oxide
    The CORRECT answer is:

    A. I, II, V   B. I, II, IV   C. II, IV
    D. II, III, IV   E. II, IV, V

23. Cumulative systemic toxicity is a health hazard of
    I. rotenone
    II. nickel carbonyl
    III. captan
    IV. silion tetrahydride
    V. tetryl

    The CORRECT answer is:

    A. I, II, V   B. I, III, V   C. I, II, IV
    D. II, IV, V   E. II, III, IV

24. Banana oil may be listed under the name of

    A. amyl acetate   B. acrolein   C. butanol
    D. carbinol   E. cresols

25. Containers of Picric Acid should be clearly marked, identifying it as a(n)

    A. explosive   B. poison
    C. flammable substance   D. concentrated acid
    E. refrigerated substance

KEY (CORRECT ANSWERS)

1. B   11. E
2. B   12. D
3. E   13. C
4. D   14. D
5. E   15. A

6. E   16. B
7. C   17. B
8. B   18. A
9. A   19. E
10. A   20. B

21. D
22. D
23. B
24. A
25. A

TEST 3

DIRECTIONS: Each question or incomplete statement is followed by several suggested answers or completions. Select the one that BEST answers the question or completes the statement. *PRINT THE LETTER OF THE CORRECT ANSWER IN THE SPACE AT THE RIGHT.*

1. Workers who handle parathion powders should

    A. wash hands frequently with water
    B. wear a barrier cream
    C. wear natural rubber gloves
    D. use neutralizing solutions
    E. not wear metallic jewelry

    1.____

2. Exposure to nuisance dust is *most likely* to result in

    A. change in the air spaces in the lungs
    B. injury to the skin or mucous membranes
    C. formation of collagen
    D. chronic poisoning
    E. none of the above

    2.____

3. A liquid that gives off an unusually toxic vapor with no discomfort during exposure is

    A. formamide   B. aniline   C. indene
    D. nickel carbonyl E. chlorobenzene

    3.____

4. Methyl bromide is an irritant to

    I. skin
    II. eyes
    III. lungs
    IV. mucous membranes
    V. gastrointestinal tract

    The CORRECT answer is:

    A. I, II, IV   B. I, III   C. III, IV
    D. I, II, III   E. I, IV

    4.____

5. Ketene is a highly irritant gas to the respiratory tract and *most closely* resembles

    A. methyl acetylene   B. arsine
    C. phosgene   D. ethylene
    E. fluorine

    5.____

6. A hydrofluoric acid burn should be water-washed until

    A. a tingling sensation is felt
    B. the skin turns white
    C. severe pain is felt
    D. the skin turns pink
    E. the skin regains its normal color

    6.____

7. Extreme caution is indicated when departing too far from the TLV for formamide because

   A. it has presented serious toxicologic hazards
   B. it decomposes to carbon monoxide
   C. it hydrolyzes very rapidly at room temperature
   D. individual tolerances greatly vary
   E. evidence supports its cumulative nature

8. Long experience with human exposures to ethyl alcohol *strongly* support the recommended TLV of _____ ppm.

   A. 100,000   B. 100   C. 10   D. 1000   E. 10,000

9. The MAIN hazard associated with cresol is

   A. chloracne
   B. simple asphyxiation
   C. skin burns
   D. methemoglobin formation
   E. cholinesterase inhibition

10. Calcium cyanamide is classified as a(n)

    A. highly volatile and flammable liquid
    B. primary irritant of the mucous membranes
    C. primary skin irritant
    D. central nervous system depressant
    E. active inhibitor of plasma cholinesterase

11. _____ has not been a proven cause of occupational disease.

    A. Beryllium   B. Aluminum   C. Nickel
    D. Antimony   E. Tungsten

12. Important carbamates include all of the following EXCEPT

    A. baygon   B. vapam   C. thiodan   D. zextran   E. thiram

13. Employees working with maleic anhydride should be instructed to report

    A. episodes of dizziness or vertigo
    B. any loss of weight
    C. signs of irritation or burning of skin, eyes, or mucous membranes
    D. any blurring of vision
    E. any difficulty in walking or feeling of weakness

14. Ethyl ether is an accident hazard because

    A. no immediate symptoms are produced
    B. confusion and changes in reflexes are induced
    C. personality changes result
    D. effects vary with individual sensitivity
    E. direct contact is not necessary for exposure to occur

15. What metal is chemically similar to both iron and nickel?

    A. Cadmium   B. Magnesium   C. Platinum
    D. Cobalt   E. Zinc

16. Industrial use of benzyl chloride includes manufacture of all of the following EXCEPT

   A. plastics
   B. perfumes
   C. rubber products
   D. dyes
   E. synthetic fannins

17. Acrylonitrile is used in the manufacture of

   A. dyes
   B. synthetic fibers
   C. fertilizers
   D. perfumes
   E. refrigerant gases

18. The health hazard of simple asphyxiation is associated with
   I. phosgene
   II. ethyl chloride
   III. carbon dioxide
   IV. acetylene
   V. ethane

   The CORRECT answer is:

   A. I, IV, V
   B. I, II, III
   C. III, IV, V
   D. II, III
   E. II, IV, V

19. Chemical poisoning from soluable uranium compounds *primarily* affects

   A. blood
   B. heart
   C. liver
   D. bone structure
   E. kidneys

20. Which of the following are both fire and health hazards?
   I. Pyridine
   II. Carbon tetrachloride
   III. Morpholine
   IV. Carbon disulfide
   V. Hydrazine

   The CORRECT answer is:

   A. I, IV
   B. II, IV
   C. I, III, V
   D. II, III, V
   E. I II, III

21. Employees handling phenol or its solution should wear protective clothing made from

   A. rubber
   B. cotton
   C. polyvinyl
   D. neoprene
   E. polyester

22. A green or black skin discoloration suggests contact with

   A. nitrogen oxide
   B. nitrobenzene
   C. oxalic acid
   D. osmium tetroxide
   E. phenol

23. Which of the following are *most likely* to develop acute nicotine poisoning?

   A. Cigarette smokers
   B. Cigar smokers
   C. Workers in tobacco processing plants
   D. Workers involved in nicotine extraction operations
   E. Users of nicotine-based insecticides

24. Methyl chloroform has found wide use as a substitute for

    A. dichlorobenzene
    B. phosphorus trichloride
    C. carbon tetrachloride
    D. propylene dichloride
    E. ethyl chlorohydrin

25. What hazard is associated with finely powdered magnesium?

    A. Fire
    B. Industrial intoxication
    C. Tissue injury
    D. Eye, nose, and throat irritation
    E. Severe poisoning

KEY (CORRECT ANSWERS)

1.	C	11.	B
2.	B	12.	C
3.	D	13.	C
4.	B	14.	B
5.	C	15.	D
6.	E	16.	C
7.	E	17.	B
8.	D	18.	C
9.	C	19.	E
10.	B	20.	A

21. A
22. D
23. E
24. C
25. A

PREPARING WRITTEN MATERIAL

PARAGRAPH REARRANGEMENT
COMMENTARY

The sentences that follow are in scrambled order. You are to rearrange them in proper order and indicate the letter choice containing the correct answer at the space at the right.

Each group of sentences in this section is actually a paragraph presented in scrambled order. Each sentence in the group has a place in that paragraph; no sentence is to be left out. You are to read each group of sentences and decide upon the best order in which to put the sentences so as to form a well-organized paragraph.

The questions in this section measure the ability to solve a problem when all the facts relevant to its solution are not given.

More specifically, certain positions of responsibility and authority require the employee to discover connection between events sometimes, apparently, unrelated. In order to do this, the employee will find it necessary to correctly infer that unspecified events have probably occurred or are likely to occur. This ability becomes especially important when action must be taken on incomplete information.

Accordingly, these questions require competitors to choose among several suggested alternatives, each of which presents a different sequential arrangement of the events. Competitors must choose the MOST logical of the suggested sequences.

In order to do so, they may be required to draw on general knowledge to infer missing concepts or events that are essential to sequencing the given events. Competitors should be careful to infer only what is essential to the sequence. The plausibility of the wrong alternatives will always require the inclusion of unlikely events or of additional chains of events which are NOT essential to sequencing the given events.

It's very important to remember that you are looking for the best of the four possible choices, and that the best choice of all may not even be one of the answers you're given to choose from.

There is no one right way to solve these problems. Many people have found it helpful to first write out the order of the sentences, as they would have arranged them, on their scrap paper before looking at the possible answers. If their optimum answer is there, this can save them some time. If it isn't, this method can still give insight into solving the problem. Others find it most helpful to just go through each of the possible choices, contrasting each as they go along. You should use whatever method feels comfortable and works for you.

While most of these types of questions are not that difficult, we've added a higher percentage of the difficult type, just to give you more practice. Usually there are only one or two questions on this section that contain such subtle distinctions that you're unable to answer confidently. And you then may find yourself stuck deciding between two possible choices, neither of which you're sure about.

PREPARING WRITTEN MATERIAL
PARAGRAPH REARRANGEMENT
EXAMINATION SECTION
TEST 1

DIRECTIONS: The following groups of sentences need to be arranged in an order that makes sense. Select the letter preceding the sequence that represents the best sentence order. *PRINT THE LETTER OF THE CORRECT ANSWER IN THE SPACE AT THE RIGHT.*

1. I. The ostrich egg shell's legendary toughness makes it an excellent substitute for certain types of dishes or dinnerware, and in parts of Africa ostrich shells are cut and decorated for use as containers for water.
    II. Since prehistoric times, people have used the enormous egg of the ostrich as a part of their diet, a practice which has required much patience and hard work—to hard boil an ostrich egg takes about four hours.
    III. Opening the egg's shell, which is rock hard and nearly an inch thick, requires heavy tools, such as a saw or chisel; from inside, a baby ostrich must use a hornlike projection on its beak as a miniature pick-axe to escape from the egg.
    IV. The offspring of all higher-order animals originate from single egg cells that are carried by mothers, and most of these eggs are relatively small, often microscopic.
    V. The egg of the African ostrich, however, weighs a massive thirty pounds, making it the largest single cell on earth, and a common object of human curiosity and wonder.
    The BEST order is:
    A. V, IV, I, II, III   B. I, IV, V, III, II   C. IV, II, III, V, I   D. IV, V, II, III, I

    1.____

2. I. Typically only a few feet high on the open sea, individual tsunami have been known to circle the entire globe two or three times if their progress is not interrupted, but are not usually dangerous until they approach the shallow water that surrounds land masses.
    II. Some of the most terrifying and damaging hazards caused by earthquakes are tsunami, which were once called "tidal waves"—a poorly chosen name, since these waves have nothing to do with tides.
    III. Then a wave, slowed by the sudden drag on the lower part of its moving water column, will pile upon itself, sometimes reaching a height of over 100 feet.
    IV. Tsunami (Japanese for "great harbor wave") are seismic waves that are caused by earthquakes near oceanic trenches, and once triggered, can travel up to 600 miles an hour on the open ocean.
    V. A land-shoaling tsunami is capable of extraordinary destruction; some tsunami have deposited large boats miles inland, washed out two-foot-thick seawalls, and scattered locomotive trains over long distances.
    The BEST order is:
    A. IV, I, III, II, V   B. I, III, IV, II, V   C. V, I, III, II, IV   D. II, IV, I, III, V

    2.____

3.
   I. Soon, by the 1940s, jazz was the most popular type of music among American intellectuals and college students.
   II. In the early days of jazz, it was considered "lowdown" music, or music that was played only in rough, disreputable bars and taverns.
   III. However, jazz didn't take too long to develop from early ragtime melodies into more complex, sophisticated forms, such as Charlie Parker's "bebop" style of jazz.
   IV. After charismatic band leaders such as Duke Ellington and Count Basie brought jazz to a larger audience, and jazz continued to evolve into more complicated forms, white audiences began to accept and even to enjoy the new American art form.
   V. Many white Americans, who then dictated the tastes of society, were wary of music that was played almost exclusively in black clubs in the poorer sections of cities and towns.

   The BEST order is:
   A. V, IV, III, II, I   B. II, V, III, IV, I   C. IV, V, III, I, II   D. I, II, IV, III, V

3._____

4.
   I. Then, hanging in a windless place, the magnetized end of the needle would always point to the south.
   II. The needle could then be balanced on the rim of a cup, or the edge of a fingernail, but this balancing act was hard to maintain, and the needle often fell off.
   III. Other needles would point to the north, and it was important for any traveler finding his way with a compass to remember which kind of magnetized needle he was carrying.
   IV. To make some of the earliest compasses in recorded history, ancient Chinese "magicians" would rub a needle with a piece of magnetized iron called a lodestone.
   V. A more effective method of keeping the needle free to swing with its magnetic pull was to attach a strand of silk to the center of the needle with a tiny piece of wax.

   The BEST order is:
   A. IV, II, V, I, III   B. IV, III, V, II, I   C. IV, V, II, I, III   D. IV, I, III, V, II

4._____

5.
   I. The now-famous first mate of the *H.M.S. Bounty*, Fletcher Christian, founded one of the world's most peculiar civilizations in 1790.
   II. The men knew they had just committed a crime for which they could be hanged, so they set sail for Pitcairn, a remote, abandoned island in the far eastern region of the Polynesian archipelago, accompanied by twelve Polynesian women and six men.
   III. In a mutiny that has become legendary, Christian and the others forced Captain Bligh into a lifeboat and set him adrift off the coast of Tonga in April of 1789.
   IV. In early 1790, the *Bounty* landed at Pitcairn Island, where the men lived out the rest of their lives and founded an isolated community which to this day includes direct descendants of Christian and the other Crewmen.

5._____

V. The *Bounty*, commanded by Captain William Bligh, was in the middle of a global voyage, and Christian and his shipmates had come to the conclusion that Bligh was a reckless madman who would lead them to their deaths unless they took the ship from him.

The BEST order is:
A. IV, V, III, II, I   B. I, III, V, II, IV   C. I, V, III, II, IV   D. III, I, V, IV, II

6. I. But once the vines had been led to make orchids, the flowers had to be carefully hand-pollinated, because unpollinated orchids usually lasted less than a day, wilting and dropping off the vine before it had even become dark.
    II. The Totonac farmers discovered that looping a vine back around once it reached a five-foot height on its host tree would cause the vine to flower.
    III. Though they knew how to process the fruit pods and extract vanilla's flavoring agent, the Totonacs also knew that a wild vanilla vine did not produce abundant flowers or fruit.
    IV. Wild vines climbed along the trunks and canopies of trees, and this constant upward growth diverted most of the vine's energy to making leaves instead of the orchid flowers that once pollinated, would produce the flavorful pods.
    V. Hundreds of years before vanilla became a prized food flavoring in Europe and the Western World, the Totonac Indians of the Mexican Gulf Coast were skilled cultivators of the vanilla vine, whose fruit they literally worshipped as a goddess.

    The BEST order is:
    A. II, III, IV, I, V   B. II, IV, III, I, V   C. V, III, IV, II, I   D. III, IV, I, II, V

7. I. Once airborne, the spider is at the mercy of the air currents—usually the spider takes a brief journey, traveling close to the ground, but some have been found in air samples collected as high as 10,000 feet, or been reported landing on ships far out at sea.
    II. Once a young spider has hatched, it must leave the environment into which it was born as quickly as possible, in order to avoid competing with its hundreds of brothers and sisters for food.
    III. The silk rises into warm air currents, and as soon as the pull feels adequate the spider lets go and drifts up into the air, suspended from the silk strand in the same way that a person might parasail.
    IV. To help young spiders do this, many species have adapted a practice known as "aerial dispersal," or, in common speech, "ballooning."
    V. A spider that wants to leave its surroundings quickly will climb to the top of a grass system or twig, face into the wind, and aim its back end into the air, releasing a long stream of silk from the glands near the tip of its abdomen.

    The BEST order is:
    A. V, IV, II, III, I   B. V, II, IV, I, III   C. II, V, IV, III, I   D. II, IV, V, III, I

8. I. For about a year, Tycho worked at a castle in Prague with a scientist named Johannes Kepler, but their association was cut short by another argument that drove Kepler out of the castle, to later develop, on his own, the theory of planetary orbits.
    II. Tycho found life without a nose embarrassing, so he made a new nose for himself out of silver, which reportedly remained glued to his face for the rest of his life.
    III. Tycho Brahe, the 17th-century Danish astronomer, is today more famous for his odd and arrogant personality than for any contribution he has made to our knowledge of the stars and planets.
    IV. Early in his career, as a student at Rostock University, Tycho got into an argument with another student about who was the better mathematician, and the two became so angry that the argument turned into a sword fight, during which Tycho's nose was sliced off.
    V. Later in his life, Tycho's arrogance may have kept him from playing a part in one of the greatest astronomical discoveries in history: the elliptical orbits of the solar system's planets.
    The BEST order is:
    A. I, IV, II, III, V   B. IV, II, III, V, I   C. IV, II, I, III, V   D. III, IV, II, V, I

9. I. The processionaries are so used to this routine that if a person picks up the end of a silk line and brings it back to the origin—creating a closed circle—the caterpillars may travel around and around for days, sometimes starving or freezing, without changing course.
    II. Rather than relying on sight or sound, the other caterpillars, who are lined up end-to-end behind the leader, travel to and from their nests by walking on this silk line, and each will reinforce it by laying down its own marking line as it passes over.
    III. In order to insure the safety of individuals, the processionary caterpillar nests in a tree with dozens of other caterpillars, and at night, when it is safest, they all leave together in search of food.
    IV. The processionary caterpillar of the European continent is a perfect illustration of how much some inspect species rely on instinct in their daily routines.
    V. As they leave their nests, the processionaries form a single-file line behind a leader who spins and lays out a silk line to mark the chosen path.
    The BEST order is:
    A. IV, III, V, II, I   B. III, V, IV, II, I   C. III, V, II, I, IV   D. IV, V, III, I, II

10. I. Often, the child is also given a handcrafted walker or push cart, to provide support for its first upright explorations.
    II. In traditional Indian families, a child's first steps are celebrated as a ceremonial event, rooted in ancient myth.
    III. These carts are often intricately designed to resemble the chariot of Krishna, an important figure in Indian mythology.
    IV. The sound of these anklet bells is intended to mimic the footsteps of the legendary child Rama, who is celebrated in devotional songs throughout India.

V. When the child's parents see that the child is ready to begin walking, they will fit it with specially designed ankle bracelets, adorned with gently ringing bells.

The BEST order is:
A. II, III, IV, I, V   B. II, V, III, I, IV   C. V, IV, I, III, II   D. V, III, II, I, IV

11. I. The settlers planted Osage oranges all across Middle America, and today long lines and rectangles of Osage orange trees can still be seen on the prairies, running along the former boundaries of farms that no longer exist.
II. After trying sod walls and water-filled ditches with no success, American farmers began to look for a plant that was adaptable to prairie weather, and that could be trimmed into a hedge that was "pig-tight, horse-high, and bull-strong."
III. The tree, so named because it bore a large (but inedible) fruit the size of an orange, was among the sturdiest and hardiest of American trees, and was prized among Native Americans for the strength and flexibility of bows which were made from its wood.
IV. The first people to practice agriculture on the American flatlands were faced with an important problem: what would they use to fence their land in a place that was almost entirely without trees or rocks?
V. Finally, an Illinois farmer brought the settlers a tree that was native to the land between the Red and Arkansas rivers, a tree called the Osage orange.

The BEST order is:
A. II, I, V, III, IV   B. I, II, III, IV, V   C. IV, II, V, III, I   D. IV, II, I, III, V

11.____

12. I. After about ten minutes of such spirited and complicated activity, the head dancer is free to make up his or her own movements while maintaining the interest of the New Year's crowd.
II. The dancer will then perform a series of leg kicks, while at the same time operating the lion's mouth with his own hand and moving the ears and eyes by means of a string which is attached to the dancer's own mouth.
III. The most difficult role of this dance belongs to the one who controls the lion's head; this person must lead all the other "parts" of the lion through the choreographed segments of the dance.
IV. The head dancer begins with a complex series of steps. alternately stepping forward with the head raised, and then retreating a few steps while lowering the head, a movement that is intended to create the impression that the lion is keeping a watchful eye for anything evil.
V. When performing a traditional Chinese New Year's lion dance, several performers must fit themselves inside a large lion costume and work together to enact different parts of the dance.

The BEST order is:
A. V, III, IV, II, I   B. III, IV, II, V, I   C. III, I, V, IV, II   D. IV, II, III, V, I

12.____

13. I. For many years the shell of the chambered nautilus was treasured in Europe for its beauty and intricacy, but collectors were unaware that they were in possession of the structure that marked a "missing link" in the evolution of marine mollusks.
II. The nautilus, however, evolved a series of enclosed chambers in its shell, and invented a new use for the structure: the shell began to serve as a buoyancy device.
III. Equipped with this new flotation device, the nautilus did not need the single, muscular foot of its predecessors, but instead developed flaps, tentacles, and a gentle form of jet propulsion that transformed it into the first mollusk able to take command of its own density and explore a three-dimensional world.
IV. By pumping and adjusting air pressure into the chambers, the nautilus could spend the day resting on the bottom, and then rise toward the surface at night in search of food.
V. The nautilus shell looks like a large snail shell, similar to those of its ancestors, who used their shells as protective coverings while they were anchored to the sea floor.
The BEST order is:
A. V, II, IV, I, III   B. V, I, II, III, IV   C. I, II, V, III, IV   D. I, V, II, IV, III

14. I. While France and England battled for control of the region, the Acadiens prospered on the fertile farmland, which was finally secured by England in 1713.
II. Early in the 17th century, settlers from Western France founded a colony called Acadie in what is now the Canadian province of Nova Scotia.
III. At this time, English officials feared the presence of spies among the Acadiens who might be loyal to their French homeland, and the Acadiens were deported to spots along the Atlantic and Caribbean shores of America.
IV. The French settlers remained on this land, under English rule, for around forty years, until the beginning of the French and Indian War, another conflict between France and England.
V. As the Acadien refugees drifted toward a final home in Southern Louisiana, neighbors shortened their name to "Cadien," and finally "Cajun," the name which the descendants of early Acadiens still call themselves.
The BEST order is:
A. I, IV, II, III, V   B. II, I, III, V, IV   C. II, I, IV, III, V   D. V, II, III, IV, I

15. I. Traditional households in the Eastern and Western regions of Africa serve two meals a day—one at around noon, and the other in the evening.
II. The starch is then used in the way that Americans might use a spoon, to scoop up a portion of the main dish on the person's plate.
III. The reason for the starch's inclusion in every meal has to do with taste as well as nutrition; African food can be very spicy, and the starch is known to cool the burning effect of the main dish.
IV. When serving these meals, the main dish is usually served on individual plates, and the starch is served on a communal plate, from which diners break off a piece of bread or scoop rice or fufu in their fingers.

V. The typical meals usually consist of a thick stew or soup as the main course, and an accompanying starch—either bread, rice, or *fufu*, a starchy grain paste similar in consistency to mashed potatoes.
The BEST order is:
A. V, II, III, IV, I B. V, I, IV, III, II C. I, IV, V, III, II D. I, V, IV, II, III

16.
I. In the early days of the American Midwest, Indiana settlers sometimes came together to hold an event called an apple peeling, where neighboring settlers gathered at the homestead of a host family to help prepare the hosts' apple crop for cooking, canning, and making apple butter.
II. At the beginning of the event, each peeler sat down in front of a ten- or twenty-gallon stone jar and was given a crock of apples and a paring knife.
III. Once a peeler had finished with a crock, another was placed next to him; if the peeler was an unmarried man, he kept a strict count of the number of apples he had peeled, because the winner was allowed to kiss the girl of his choice.
IV. The peeling usually ended by 9:30 in the evening, when the neighbors gathered in the host family's parlor for a dance social.
V. The apples were peeled, cored, and quartered, and then placed into the jar.
The BEST order is:
A. I, V, III, IV, II B. II, V, III, IV, I C. I, II, V, III, IV D. II, I, V, IV, III

16.____

17.
I. If your pet turtle is a land turtle and is native to temperate climates, it will stop eating some time in October, which should be your cue to prepare the turtle for hibernation.
II. The box should then be covered with a wire screen, which will protect the turtle from any rodents or predators that might want to take advantage of a motionless and helpless animal.
III. When your turtle hasn't eaten for a while and appears ready to hibernate, it should be moved to its winter quarters, most likely a cellar or garage, where the temperature should range between 40° and 45°F.
IV. Instead of feeding the turtle, you should bathe it every day in warm water, to encourage the turtle to empty its intestines in preparation for its long winter sleep.
V. Here the turtle should be placed in a well-ventilated box whose bottom is covered with a moisture-absorbing layer of clay beads, and then filled three-fourths full with almost dry peat moss or wood chips, into which the turtle will burrow and sleep for several months.
The BEST order is:
A. I, IV, III, V, II B. III, IV, II, V, I C. III, II, IV, I, V D. IV, V, II, III, I

17.____

18.
I. Once he has reached the nest, the hunter uses two sturdy bamboo poles like huge chopsticks to pull the next away from the mountainside, into a large basket that will be lowered to people waiting below.
II. The world's largest honeybees colonize the Nealese mountainsides, building honeycombs as large as a person on sheer rock faces that are often hundreds of feet high.

18.____

III. In the remote mountain country of Nepal, a small band of "honey hunters" carry out a tradition so ancient that 10,000 year-old drawings of the practice have been found in the caves of Nepal.
IV. To harvest the honey and beeswax from these combs, a honey hunter climbs above the nests, lowers a long bamboo-fiber ladder over the cliff, and then climbs down.
V. Throughout this dangerous practice, the hunter is stung repeatedly, and only the veterans, with skin that has been toughened over the years, are able to return from a hunt without the painful swelling caused by stings.

The BEST order is:
   A. II, IV, III, V, I   B. II, IV, I, V, III   C. V, III, II, IV, I   D. III, II, IV, I, V

19. I. After the Romans left Britain, there were relentless attacks on the islands from the barbarian tribes of northern Germany—the Angles, Saxons, and Jutes.
II. As the empire weakened, Roman soldiers withdrew from Britain, leaving behind a country that continued to practice the Christian religion that had been introduced by the Romans.
III. Early Latin writings tell of a Christian warrior named Arturius (Arthur, in English) who led the British citizens to defeat these barbarian invades, and brought an extended period of peace to the lands of Britain.
IV. Long ago, the British Isles were part of the far-flung Roman Empire that extended across most of Europe and into Africa and Asia.
V. The romantic legend of King Arthur and his knights of the Round Table, one of the most popular and widespread stories of all time, appears to have some foundation in history.

The BEST order is:
   A. V, IV, III, II, I   B. V, IV, II, I, III   C. IV, V, II, III, I   D. IV, III, II, I, V

20. I. The cylinder was allowed to cool until it could stand on its own, and then it was cut from the tube and split down the side with a single straight cut.
II. Nineteenth-century glassmakers, who had not yet discovered the glazier's modern techniques for making panes of glass, had to create a method for converting their blown gas into flat sheets.
III. The bubble was then pierced at the end to make a hole that opened up while the glassmaker gently spun it, creating a cylinder of glass.
IV. Turned on its side and laid on a conveyor belt, the cylinder was strengthened, or tempered, by being heated again and cooled very slowly, eventually flattening out into a single rectangular of glass.
V. To do this, the glassmaker dipped the end of a long tube into melted glass and blew into the other end of the tube, creating an expanding bubble of glass.

The BEST order is:
   A. II, V, III, IV, I   B. II, IV, V, III, I   C. III, V, II, IV, I   D. III, I, IV, V, II

21.
   I. The splints are almost always hidden, but horses are occasionally born whose splinted toes project from the leg on either side, just above the hoof.
   II. The second and fourth toes remained, but shrank to thin splints of bone that fused invisibly to the horse's leg bone.
   III. Horses are unique among mammals, having evolved feet that each end in what is essentially a single toe, capped by a large, sturdy hoof.
   IV. Julius Caesar, an emperor of ancient Rome, was said to have owned one of these three-toed horses, and considered it so special that he would not permit anyone else to ride it.
   V. Though the horse's earlier ancestors possessed the traditional mammalian set of five toes on each foot, the horse has retained only its third toe; its first and fifth toes disappeared completely as the horse evolved.
   The BEST order is:
   A. III, V, II, I, IV   B. V, III, II, IV, I   C. III, II, V, I, IV   D. V, II, III, I, IV

22.
   I. The new building materials—some of which are twenty feet long, and weigh nearly six tons—were transported to Pohnpei on rafts, and were brought into their present position by using hibiscus fiber ropes and leverage to move the stone columns upward along the inclined trunks of coconut palm trees.
   II. The ancestors built great fires to heat the stone, and then poured cool seawater on the columns, which caused the stone to contract and split along natural fracture lines.
   III. The now-abandoned enclave of Nan Madol, a group of 92 man-made islands off the shore of the Micronesian island of Pohnpei, is estimated to have been built around the year 500 A.D.
   IV. The islanders say their ancestors quarried stone columns from a nearby island, where large basalt columns were formed by the cooling of molten lava.
   V. The structures of Nan Madol are remarkable for the sheer size of some of the stone "longs" or columns that were used to create the walls of the offshore community, and today anthropologists can only rely on the information of existing local people for clues about how Nan Madol was built.
   The BEST order is:
   A. V, IV, III, II, I   B. V, III, I, IV, II   C. III, V, IV, II, I   D. III, I, IV, II, V

23.
   I. One of the most easily manipulated substances on earth, glass can be made into ceramic tiles that are composed of over 90% air.
   II. NASA's space shuttles are the first spacecraft ever designed to leave and re-enter the earth's atmosphere while remaining intact.
   III. These ceramic tiles are such effective insulators that when a tile emerges from the oven in which it was fired, it can be held safely in a person's hand by the edges while its interior still glows at a temperature well over 2000°F.
   IV. Eventually, the engineers were led to a material that is as old as our most ancient civilization.
   V. Because the temperature during atmospheric re-entry is so incredibly hot, it took NASA's engineers some time to find a substance capable of protecting the shuttles.

The BEST order is:
A. V, II, I, II, IV   B. II, V, IV, I, III   C. II, III, I, IV, V   D. V, IV, III, I, II

24. I. The secret to teaching any parakeet to talk is patience, and the understanding that when a bird talks," it is simply imitating what it hears, rather than putting ideas into words.
II. You should stay just out of sight of the bird and repeat the phrase you want it to learn, for at least fifteen minutes every morning and evening.
III. It is important to leave the bird without any words of encouragement or farewell; otherwise it might combine stray remarks or phrases, such as "Good night," with the phrase you are trying to teach it.
IV. For this reason, to train your bird to imitate your words you should keep it free of any distractions, especially other noises, while you are giving it "lesson."
V. After your repetition, you should quietly leave the bird alone for a while, to think over what it has just heard.
The BEST order is:
A. I, IV, II, V, III   B. I, II, IV, III, V   C. III, II, I, V, IV   D. III, I, V, IV, II

24.____

25. I. As a school approaches, fishermen from neighboring communities join their fishing boats together as a fleet, and string their gill nets together to make a huge fence that is held up by cork floats.
II. At a signal from the party leaders, or *nakura*, the family members pound the sides of the boats or beat the water with long poles, creating a sudden and deafening noise.
III. The fishermen work together to drag the trap into a half-circle that may reach 300 yards in diameter, and then the families move their boats to form the other half of the circle around the school of fish.
IV. The school of fish flee from the commotion into the awaiting trap, where a final wall of net is thrown over the open end of the half-circle, securing the day's haul.
V. Indonesian people from the area around the Sulu islands live on the sea, in floating villages made of lashed-together or stilted homes, and make much of their living by fishing their home waters for migrating schools of snapper, scad, and other fish.
The BEST order is:
A. I, V, III, IV, II   B. I, II, IV, III, V   C. V, I, II, III, IV   D. V, I, III, II, IV

25.____

KEY (CORRECT ANSWERS)

1.	D	11.	C
2.	D	12.	A
3.	B	13.	D
4.	A	14.	C
5.	C	15.	D
6.	C	16.	C
7.	D	17.	A
8.	D	18.	D
9.	A	19.	B
10.	B	20.	A

21. A
22. C
23. B
24. A
25. D

PREPARING WRITTEN MATERIAL
EXAMINATION SECTION
TEST 1

DIRECTIONS: Each short paragraph below is followed by four restatements or summaries of the information contained within it. Select the one that most completely and accurately states the information or opinion given in the paragraph. *PRINT THE LETTER OF THE CORRECT ANSWER IN THE SPACE AT THE RIGHT.*

1. Australia's koalas live solely on a diet of the leaves of the eucalyptus tree, a low-protein food that requires a koala to eat about three or four pounds of leaves a day. For most mammals, these strong-smelling leaves, saturated with toxins such as phenols and the oily compound known as cineole, are among the least digestible foods on the planet. However, the koala is equipped with a digestive system that is able to handle these toxins, trapping the tiniest leaf particles for as much as eight days while the sugars, proteins, and fats are extracted.
    A. Because eucalyptus leaves contain a large amount of toxins and oils, it takes a long time for koalas to digest them.
    B. Koalas have to eat three or four pounds of eucalyptus leaves a day, because the leaves are so poor in nutrients.
    C. Koalas have a unique digestive system that allows them to exist solely on a diet of eucalyptus leaves, which are generally toxic and inedible.
    D. The digestive system of the koala illustrates the unique evolutionary palette of the Australian continent.

1._____

2. Norway's special geopolitical position—it was the only NATO country to share a border with Russia—drove it to adopt much more cautious policies than other European countries during the Cold War. Its decision to join NATO led to strong protests from Russia, and in order to avoid provocation, Norway's foreign policy had to balance the need for ensuring defense capability with the need to keep tensions at the lowest possible level. Norway's low-tension "base policy" made clear the nation's refusal to allow foreign military forces on Norwegian territory as long as the country is not attacked or threatened with an attack.
    A. Norway's "base policy," in spite of its shared border with Russia, is the work of a pacifist nation that should serve as a model for foreign diplomacy everywhere.
    B. When Norway joined NATO, Russia feared a ground invasion over their shared border.
    C. The "base policy" of Norway is a perfect illustration on how much of Europe during the Cold War was a powder keg ready to explode at the slightest provocation.
    D. As the only member of the NATO alliance to border on Russia, Norway was forced to adopt a more conciliatory foreign policy than other members of the alliance.

2._____

3. During the women's suffrage movement of the early twentieth century, it was   3.____
typical of many psychologists and anti-suffragists to automatically associate
feminism with mental illness. In 1918, H.W. Frink wrote of feminists: "A certain
proportion of at least the most militant suffragists are neurotics who in some
instances are compensating for masculine trends, in others, are more or less
successfully sublimating sadistic and homosexual ones." In the United States,
anti-suffragists, finding comfort in psychology, concluded that suffragists all
bordered hysteria and, thus, their arguments could not be taken seriously,
   A. The relationship between suffragism and feminism led many scientists to
      conclude that suffragists were afflicted with some kinds of mental illness.
   B. During the women's suffrage movement, anti-suffragists such as H.W.
      Frink tended to label women who fought for voting rights as mentally ill in
      order to dismiss their arguments.
   C. Responses to the women's suffrage movement are indicative of the
      tendency to label those who challenge the status quo as "Crazy" than to
      comfort their arguments.
   D. Most of the women who fought for suffrage during the early twentieth
      century were feminists who were mentally ill.

4. All of the earth's early plant life lived in the ocean, and most of these plants were   4.____
concentrated in the shallow coastal waters, where the sun's energy could be
easily absorbed. Because of the constant advance and retreat of tides in these
regions, the plants—mostly algae—were repeatedly exposed to the
atmosphere, and were forced to adapt to life out of water. It took millions of
years before plant species had evolved that could survive out of the sea
altogether, with stems that drew water from the ground, and a waxy covering to
keep them from drying in the sun.
   A. After spending millions of years underwater, the earth's plants finally
      evolved ways of surviving on land.
   B. Most algaes today, because of evolutionary advances, are able to survive
      for extended periods of time out of water.
   C. Despite the fact that plants began as purely underwater organisms, they
      have always needed the sun's energy to survive.
   D. Land plants evolved from sea plants after millions of years in response to
      the gradual warming of the earth's atmosphere.

5. Because of the unique convergence of mild temperature and abundant rain   5.____
(17 feet a year), British Columbia's temperate coastal rainforest is the most
biologically productive ecosystem on earth. It's also an increasingly rare and
vulnerable ecosystem: in its Holocene heyday, it covered only 0.2 percent of
the earth's land surface. Today, logging and other development have
consumed more than half this original range.
   A. The uniquely productive ecosystem of British Columbia's coastal
      rainforest has always been small, and has been reduced by human
      activity.
   B. Despite the fact that it is the most biologically productive ecosystem on
      earth, the coastal rainforest of British Columbia has been largely ignored
      by environmental activists.

C. The coastal rainforests of British Columbia have been nearly devastated by logging and other development.
D. British Columbia's coastal rainforest originated during the Holocene Era, but has declined steadily ever since.

6. The Roman Empire, which ruled much of the Western world for hundreds of years, was led by an aristocratic class famous for its tendency to drink large amounts of wine. Recently, an American medical researcher theorized that this taste for wine was eventually what caused the decline and fall of the empire—not the drinking of the wine itself, but a gradual poisoning from the lead that was used to line and seal Roman wine casks. The researcher, Dr. S.C. Gilfillan, argues that this lead poisoning specifically affected members of the Empire's ruling class, because they were the Romans most likely to consume wine and other products, like preserved fruits, that were stored in lead-lined jars.   6._____
    A. The Roman aristocracy's taste for wine and dried fruits, according to one researcher, is a cautionary tale about the consequences of overindulgence.
    B. While the Roman Empire's ruling class suffered from widespread lead poisoning, most commoners remained in good health throughout the empire.
    C. One of the most far-fetched theories about the fall of the Roman Empire concerns itself with the lead used to line the wine casks and fruit jars of the ruling class.
    D. An American medical researcher has theorized that the fall of the Roman Empire was caused by slow poisoning from the lead used to line and seal Roman wine casks and fruit jars.

7. In the second century B.C., King Hiero of Syracuse called upon the renowned scientist, Archimedes, to find a way to see if his crown was made of pure gold or a combination of metals. Archimedes came upon the solution some time later, as he was entering a tub full of hot water and noticed that the weight of his body displaced a certain amount of water. Realizing that this same principle could be used on the crown, he forgot himself with excitement, jumping out of the tub and running naked through the town, yelling "Eureka! Eureka!"   7._____
    A. Archimedes, in making his famous discovery, unknowingly contributed the word "Eureka!" to the English vocabulary.
    B. The relative purity of gold can be determined by the amount of water it displaces when submerged.
    C. Archimedes, after discovering the solution to a scientific problem while stepping into his tub, became so excited that he ran through the town naked.
    D. The word "Eureka" has become a part of the English language because of an interesting story involving the ancient scientist, Archimedes.

8. In the nineteenth century most Americans had never heard of, let alone tasted, an abalone, the marine mollusk considered to be a delicacy by many Asians, and undisturbed abalone populations thrived all along the west coast. When the California Gold Rush of the 1840s and 1850s brought thousands of Asian   8._____

immigrants to America, many of these people began to harvest the dense beds of abalone that inhabited the state's intertidal zone. The Asian harvests eventually brought in annual catches of over 4 million pounds of abalone, and as a result, some county governments passed ordinances making it illegal to dive for abalone in waters less than twenty feet deep.
- A. The Asians who immigrated to California during the Gold Rush harvested so much abalone from intertidal waters that some governments were compelled to limit abalone diving.
- B. Abalone diving was unheard of in California before the Gold Rush, when many Asians immigrated to the state and began to harvest abalone from the intertidal zone.
- C. The extreme shortage of abalone in California's intertidal waters can be traced to the Asians who immigrated during the Gold Rush.
- D. The abalone of California's coastal waters generally live in waters less than twenty feet deep, where they are not protected by most county governments.

9. Maria Tallchief, the daughter of a full-blood Osage Indian from Oklahoma, was America's first internationally celebrated prima ballerina, rising to stardom at a time when classical American ballet was still struggling to gain international acceptance and acclaim. Her innovative interpretations of such classics as "Swan Lake" and "The Nutcracker" helped convince critics worldwide that American ballet was a force to be reckoned with, and her glamorous beauty helped popularize ballet in America at a time when very few people took it seriously.
    - A. As ballet grew more popular in America, Maria Tallchief became a phenomenon in Europe, helping to secure a worldwide reputation for excellence for American ballet.
    - B. Nobody in America took ballet seriously until the beautiful Maria Tallchief became an international star.
    - C. With her beauty and technical innovations, Maria Tallchief gained unprecedented critical and popular success for American ballet.
    - D. Before the success of Maria Tallchief, there were not many ballet dancers in the United States worth noticing.

9.____

10. Early in the Constitutional Convention of 1787, the idea of a two-tiered legislature was agreed upon by the framers of the Constitution. The final form of each of the resulting houses, however, was an issue that was debated openly, and which was finally resolved by the "great compromise" of the Constitutional Convention. While the House of Representatives was intended to be a large, politically sensitive body, the Senate was designed to be a moderating influence that would check the powers of the House.
    - A. The framers of the Constitution could not agree on whether the nation's legislature should be bicameral, or two-tiered, at first, but after the "great compromise," they devised a House and Senate.
    - B. The Constitutional Convention of 1787 ended with the "great compromise" that gave the nation its two-tiered legislature.

10.____

C. After much behind-the-scenes dealmaking, the two-tiered legislature of the United States was devised by the framers of the Constitution.
D. The framers of the Constitution, after some debate, decided on a two-tiered legislature made up of a House of Representatives and a Senate that was less susceptible to regional politics.

11. Although scientists have succeeded in creating robots able to process huge amounts of information, they are still struggling to create one whose reasoning ability matches that of a human baby. The main challenge facing these scientists is the difficulty of understanding and imitating the complex process of human perception and reasoning, which involve the ability to register and analyze even the smallest changes in the external environment, and then to act on those changes.

    11.____

    A. Even the most sophisticated robot is unable to imitate innate human abilities such as learning to walk, converse, or perceive depth.
    B. Because of their inability to process large amounts of information, robots have yet to achieve even the most fundamental level of reasoning.
    C. Despite considerable technological advances, scientists have as yet been unable to produce a robot that can respond intelligently to changes in its environment.
    D. Because robots cannot automatically filter out all extraneous information and focus on the most important details of a given situation, they are unable to reason as well as humans.

12. Thor Heyerdahl, a Norwegian anthropologist, had long held the opinion that the Polynesian inhabitants of South Pacific islands such as Samoa, Tonga, and Fiji had actually been migrants from South America. To prove that this was possible, in1947 Heyerdahl made a crude raft out of balsa wood, which he named after an Incan sun god, *Kon-Tiki*, and sailed from the coast of Peru to the islands east of Tahiti.

    12.____

    A. Thor Heyerdahl's 1947 voyage on the *Kon-Tiki* proved that Polynesians probably had common ancestors in South America.
    B. While Thor Heyerdahl's *Kon-Tiki* voyage suggested a South American origin for Polynesians, most experts today believe the great migrations were launched from somewhere near Indonesia.
    C. To support the idea that Polynesians could have sailed from South America to the Pacific Islands, Thor Heyerdahl sailed the *Kon-Tiki* from Peru to Tahiti in 1947.
    D. Thor Heyerdahl's famous raft, the *Kon-Tiki*, was named for an Incan sun god, and was so well-made that it made it from Peru to Tahiti.

13. During the Age of Exploration, after thousands of miles of open sea, ships entered the bays of the Azore Islands, west of Portugal, with tattered sails, battered hulls, crewmen weakened from scurvy, and cargo holds laden with the treasure they had gained on their long trading journeys. Spanish, English, and Dutch warships prowled the waters around the Azores to protect this treasure, sometimes even sinking their own ships to keep it from falling into enemy

    13.____

hands. During these fierce battles, many ships filled with treasure were sent to the ocean floor, where they still remain, preserved by the cold saltwater and centuries of rest.
- A. Although they are now sparsely populated, the Azore Islands were once a resting place for every ship returning from a long journey to the Americas.
- B. Many treasure hunters and archaeologists believe the sea floor around the Azores, a group of islands west of Portugal, still harbors some of the richest sunken treasure in the world.
- C. Economic competition between the European powers was so intense during the Age of Exploration that captains would rather sink their own ships rather than let their treasure fall into enemy hands.
- D. The rich history of the Azore Islands has deposited a large amount of sunken treasure in their surrounding waters.

14. The Whigs, a short-lived American political party, were wary of a domineering president, and many of them believed that the legislative branch should govern the nation. In particular, Whig leader Henry Clay often attempted to bully and belittle President John Tyler into submission. Tyler's resistance to Clay's high-handed tactics strengthened the office of the presidency, and in particular gave greater credibility to all later vice presidents who happened to succeed to the office.   14.____
    - A. While U.S. politics was at first dominated by the legislature, President John Tyler shifted the center of power to the presidency, while laying the groundwork for the downfall of the Whig Party.
    - B. President John Tyler, a failure by almost any other measure, can at least be credited with contributing to the strength of the presidency.
    - C. Henry Clay, who believed in a strong legislature, failed to win much influence over presidents who were not from the Whig Party.
    - D. President John Tyler, in resisting Henry Clay's bullying tactics, strengthened the U.S. presidency and lent credibility to the authority of vice presidential successors to the presidency.

15. By far the richest city on earth, Tokyo, Japan is also one of the most over-crowded; most of its people are only able to afford living in extremely small houses and apartments. In addition to cramped housing, Tokyo's overpopulation has created a commuter problem so grim that a corps of "pushers" has been hired by the city, to stand outside crowded commuter trains and help pack people inside. Problems such as these are so severe in Tokyo that there has been serious talk in recent years of moving Japan's capital elsewhere.   15.____
    - A. Despite the example of Tokyo, there is no evidence to suggest that economic wealth and overpopulation are related variables.
    - B. Tokyo's prosperity has led to such overcrowding that the country of Japan has recently begun to consider moving its capital to another location.
    - C. Despite being the richest city on earth, Tokyo, Japan is seriously overcrowded.
    - D. The small houses and apartments in Tokyo, along with its overcrowded transit system, are a perfect example of how economic wealth does not always improve a society's quality of life.

16. One of the greatest, and least publicized, legacies of Native American culture   16._____
has been the worldwide cultivation of food staples through careful farming
methods. Over centuries, tribes throughout North and South America
domesticated the wild plants that have come to produce over half of the
vegetables the world eats today. Corn, or maize, was first cultivated in the
Mexican highlands almost seven thousand years ago, from a common wild
grass called teosinte, and both potatoes and tomatoes were originally
domesticated by the Peruvian Incas from native plants that still grow
throughout Peru and Bolivia.
    A. Explorers of the Americas carried many native vegetables back to
       Europe, where they continued to adapt and flourish over the centuries.
    B. Today's common corn is a descendent of the wild Mexican teosinte plant,
       and potatoes and tomatoes were originally grown by the Incas.
    C. Without the agricultural knowledge and skill of early Native Americans,
       much of the world today would be in danger of famine.
    D. Foods that are today grown and eaten almost worldwide, such as corn,
       tomatoes, and potatoes, were first cultivated by the natives of North and
       South Americas.

17. America's transportation sector—95 percent of it driven by oil—consumes   17._____
two-thirds of the petroleum used in the United States. With the 400 million cars
now on the world's roads expected to grow to 1 billion by the year 2020, oil-
foreign or not and other finite fossil-fuel resources will some day be
conversation pieces for the nostalgic, rather than components of the nation's
energy mix.
    A. In the future, most motor vehicles in the United States will be powered by
       an alternative energy source such as hydrogen or solar power.
    B. The continued growth of the oil-dependent transportation sector is
       outpacing the capacity of fossil-fuel energy resources.
    C. Our nation's dependence on foreign oil is a serious vulnerability that can
       only be corrected by increased domestic production.
    D. In the future, 1 billion cars across the world will be competing for oil and
       gasoline.

18. Althea Gibson, the first African-American to win the Wimbledon Tennis   18._____
Championship, began her career by riding the subway out of her neighborhood
in Harlem to 143rd Street, where she played paddle tennis against anyone who
dared to challenge her. Since the Wimbledon tournament was played on
grass, Gibson knew she would have to prepare herself by training on a surface
that returned balls as quickly as a grass court. She found the solution to this
problem in the gyms of Harlem, whose wood floors allowed her to perfect the
rapid volley that helped her win two Wimbledon championships.
    A. Althea Gibson's tennis skills, including her famous volley, were developed
       in and around the inner-city neighborhood of Harlem.
    B. Althea Gibson had to leave her neighborhood to learn tennis, but to
       perfect her game, she had to return home to Harlem.
    C. Without the wood floors in the gyms of her Harlem neighborhood, Althea
       Gibson probably wouldn't have developed a volley that would help her
       win two Wimbledon tennis championships.

D. Although Althea Gibson achieved international fame as the first African-American to win the Wimbledon Tennis Championship, the path she followed to that championship was as unorthodox as the champion herself.

19. The greenhouse effect is a naturally occurring process that aids in heating the Earth's surface and atmosphere. It results from the fact that certain atmospheric gases, such as carbon dioxide, water vapor, and methane, are able to change the energy balance of the planet by being able to absorb longwave radiation from the Earth's surface. Without the greenhouse effect, life on this planet would probably not exist, as the average temperature of the Earth would be a chilly 5 degrees, rather than the present 59 degrees. 19.____
    A. The naturally-occurring greenhouse effect, by which atmospheric air is warmed, enables life to exist on earth.
    B. The greenhouse effect is a completely natural phenomenon that has nothing to do with human activity, and in fact it is beneficial to the planet's ecosystems.
    C. Human contributions to the increases in the greenhouse effect threaten life on Earth.
    D. In order for life to exist on Earth there must be some kind of greenhouse effect.

20. The religious and scientific communities have for centuries been at odds with each other, and held opposing viewpoints concerning the origin and nature of life. Progressive thinkers from both groups, however, claim that the two communities, in their ways of seeking answers to humanity's most important questions, share a common set of goals and procedures that would benefit greatly from a cooperative effort. 20.____
    A. Scientists and theologians will probably never agree on the origin and nature of life, though some progressive thinkers are trying to change the way the two communities talk about these issues.
    B. Though most scientists do not believe in God, progressive religious thinkers are continually trying to persuade them otherwise.
    C. Progressive religious and scientific thinkers have identified shared goals and questions that the two communities can work together to achieve and solve.
    D. Religious thinkers, who usually scorn such scientific theories as evolution, have begun to acknowledge the usefulness of science in answering important questions.

21. The administrations of Presidents Richard Nixon and Jimmy Carter oversaw an Export-Import Bank that was increasingly active in trade promotion, with expanding programs and lending authority. During this period, expenditures for program activities expanded to five times their 1969 rate, but the bank's net income dropped sharply—the low interest rates at which the bank financed its loan programs were lowering its profits. 21.____
    A. During the Nixon and Carter administrations, the budget of the Export-Import Bank grew to five times its 1969 expenditures.

B. Though the Export-Import Bank was very active during the Nixon and Carter administrations, its profits were reduced by its low interest rates.
C. Both the Nixon and Carter administrations demonstrated a lack of fiscal discipline that led to a declining net income at the Export-Import Bank.
D. Presidents Nixon and Carter both favored an activist Export-Import Bank, but while Nixon emphasized the function of trade promotion, Carter was more focused on making loans.

22. The Kombai and Korawai tribes of eastern Indonesia are known as the "tree people" for their custom of living in large tree houses, built as high as 150 feet above ground to avoid attacks from their enemies. These houses are built mostly from the fronds of the sago palm, a plant that also serves to produce one of the tree people's primary food sources—the larvae, or grub, of the scarab beetle. The tree people cultivate grubs by cutting a stretch of sago forest and then, after splitting and tying the palms together, leaving the palms to rot.   22.____
    A. The food-gathering methods of the Kombai and Korawai illustrate that deforestation is not a contemporary problem.
    B. The Kombai and Korawai people of eastern Indonesia relay on the sago palm for both food and housing.
    C. The Kombai and Korawai fears of enemy attacks have led them to build their trees high in the forest canopy
    D. Among the world's least-tamed native cultures are the Kombai and Korawai of Irian Jaya, the easternmost region of Indonesia.

23. It's no secret that corporate and federal information networks continue to deal with increasing bandwidth needs. The appetite for data—whether it's for internet access, file delivery, or the integration of digital voice applications—isn't likely to level off any time soon, and most information technology professionals allow that there is cause for concern. But emerging technologies for increasing raw bandwidth, accompanied by the streaming and maturing of transfer and switching protocols, are a good bet to accommodate the hunger for bandwidth, at least into the near future.   23.____
    A. There are two ways to decrease the demand for more bandwidth over computer networks: either increase the "raw" amount of bandwidth over an infrastructure, or devise more efficient transfer and switching protocols.
    B. Emerging technologies, aimed at the constantly increasing demand for bandwidth, are some day likely to result in virtually unlimited bandwidth for computer networks.
    C. Many different applications contribute to the demand for bandwidth over a computer network, and so the technologies that are devised to meet this demand must be many-faceted.
    D. While there is always a need for more bandwidth on large computer networks, newer technologies promise to increase the supply in the near term.

24. In the year 805, a Japanese Buddhist monk named Dengyo Daishi returned from his studies in China with some tea seeds, which he planted on a Japanese mountainside. In China, tea had long been the favorite drink of monks, because it helped them stay awake and attentive during their long periods of meditation, and Dengyo Daishi wanted to bring this practice to Japan. Over the centuries, tea-drinking would prove to be a custom that would influence nearly every aspect of Japanese culture, and Dengyo Daishi has long been considered a sort of saint among the Japanese.

24.____

  A. Because of the cultural similarities between China and Japan, it was only a matter of time before the ritual of tea-drinking made its way from the mainland to the island empire.
  B. Dengo Daishi, the first person to plant tea seeds in Japan, is revered among today's Japanese.
  C. The Japanese tea-drinking custom was begun in 805 by a Buddhist monk who brought tea seeds from China.
  D. Without the shared cultural traditions of Buddhism, it is unlikely that tea ever would have been imported from China to Japan.

25. Aztec women held a position in society that was far more respected than that of women in most Western civilizations of the time. For example, an Aztec wife was free to divorce a man who failed to provide for their children, or who was physically abusive, and once divorced, a woman was free to remarry whomever she chose. Perhaps the unusually high regard for Aztec women is best illustrated by the traditional Aztec religious belief that a special, elevated status in the afterlife was reserved for only two types of Aztec citizens-warriors who had died defending their tribe, and woman who had died during childbirth.

25.____

  A. The rights and privileges of Aztec women demonstrate that they were more respected by their societies than women of many cultures of the time.
  B. In the Aztec culture, women had the same rights and status as the most exalted men.
  C. Though the rights of Aztec women were still generally inferior to those of men, most Aztec women were granted a high degree of independence due to their service to the community.
  D. The relatively high position that Aztec women held in their society reveals the Aztec culture to be well ahead of its time.

KEY (CORRECT ANSWERS)

1.	C	11.	C
2.	D	12.	C
3.	B	13.	D
4.	A	14.	D
5.	A	15.	B
6.	D	16.	D
7.	C	17.	B
8.	A	18.	A
9.	C	19.	A
10.	D	20.	C

21. B
22. B
23. D
24. C
25. A

———

GLOSSARY OF ENVIRONMENTAL TERMS

TABLE OF CONTENTS

	Page
Abatement ... Air Curtain	1
Air Mass ... Attrition	2
Audiometer ... Biological Oxidation	3
Biomonitoring ... Channelization	4
Chemical Oxygen Demand (COD) ... Comminution	5
Comminutor ... Detergent	6
Diatomaceous Earth (Diatomite) ... Ecological Impact	7
Ecology ... Eutrophic Lakes	8
Evaporation Ponds ... Fungi	9
Fungicide ... Hazardous Air Pollutant	10
Heat Island Effect ... Inertial Separator	11
Infiltration ... Limnology	12
Marsh ... Nuclear Power Plant	13
Nutrients ... Pathogenic	14
PCBs ... Potable Water	15
PPM ... Red Tide	16
Refuse ... Scrap	17
Screening ... Sinking	18
Skimming ... Stagnation	19
Stationary Source ... Topography	20
Toxicant ... Waste Water	21
Water Pollution ... Zooplankton	22

GLOSSARY OF ENVIRONMENTAL TERMS

A

ABATEMENT - The method of reducing the degree or intensity of pollution, also the use of such a method.

ABSORPTION - The penetration of a substance into or through another. For example, in air pollution control, absorption is the dissolving of a soluble gas, present in an emission, in a liquid which can be extracted.

ACCELERATOR - In radiology, a device for imparting high velocity to charged particles such as electrons or protons. These fast particles can penetrate matter and are known as radiation.

ACCLIMATION - The physiological and behavioral adjustments of an organism to changes in its immediate environment.

ACCLIMATIZATION - The acclimation or adaptation of a particular species over several generations to a marked change in the environment.

ACTIVATED CARBON - A highly adsorbent form of carbon, used to remove odors and toxic substances from gaseous emissions. In advanced waste treatment, activated carbon is used to remove dissolved organic matter from waste water.

ACTIVATED SLUDGE - Sludge that has been aerated and subjected to bacterial action, used to remove organic matter from sewage.

ACTIVATED SLUDGE PROCESS - The process of using biologically active sewage sludge to hasten breakdown of organic matter in raw sewage during secondary waste treatment.

ACUTE TOXICITY - Any poisonous effect produced within a short period of time, usually up to 24-96 hours, resulting in severe biological harm and often death.

ADAPTATION - A change in structure or habit of an organism that produces better adjustment to the environment.

ADSORPTION - The adhesion of a substance to the surface of a solid or liquid. Adsorption is often used to extract pollutants by causing them to be attached to such adsorbents as activated carbon or silica gel. Hydrophobic, or water-repulsing adsorbents, are used to extract oil from waterways in oil spills.

ADULTERANTS - Chemicals or substances that by law do not belong in a food, plant, animal or pesticide formulation. Adulterated products are subject to seizure by the Food and Drug Administration.

ADVANCED WASTE TREATMENT - Waste water treatment beyond the secondary or biological stage that includes removal of nutrients such as phosphorus and nitrogen and a high percentage of suspended solids. Advanced waste treatment, known as tertiary treatment, is the *polishing stage* of waste water treatment and produces a high quality effluent.

AERATION - The process of being supplied or impregnated with air. Aeration is used in waste water treatment to foster biological and chemical purification.

AEROBIC - This refers to life or processes that can occur only in the presence of oxygen.

AEROSOL - A suspension of liquid or solid particles in the air.

AFTERBURNER - An air pollution abatement device that removes undesirable organic gases through incineration.

AGRICULTURAL POLLUTION - The liquid and solid wastes from all types of farming, including runoff from pesticides, fertilizers, and feedlots; erosion and dust from plowing animal manure and carcasses and drop residues and debris. It has been estimated that agricultural pollution in the U.S. has amounted to more than 2 1/2 billion tons per year.

AIR CURTAIN - A method for mechanical containment of oil spills. Air is bubbled through a perforated pipe causing an upward water flow that retards the spreading of oil. Air curtains are also used as barriers to prevent fish from entering a polluted body of water.

AIR MASS - A widespread body of air with properties that were established while the air was situated over a particular region of the earth's surface and that undergoes specific modification while in transit away from that region.

AIR MONITORING - (See MONITORING.)

AIR POLLUTION - The presence of contaminants in the air in concentrations that prevent the normal dispersive ability of the air and that interfere directly or indirectly with man's health, safety, or comfort or with the full use and enjoyment of his property.

AIR POLLUTION EPISODE - The occurrence of abnormally high concentrations of air pollutants usually due to low winds and temperature inversion and accompanied by an increase in illness and death. (See INVERSION.)

AIR QUALITY CONTROL REGION - An area designated by the Federal government where two or more communities - either in the same or different states - share a common air pollution problem. AIR QUALITY CRITERIA - The levels of pollution and lengths of exposure at which adverse effects on health and welfare occur.

AIR QUALITY STANDARDS - The prescribed level of pollutants in the outside air that cannot be exceeded legally during a specified time in a specified geographical area.

ALGAL BLOOM - A proliferation of living algae on the surface of lakes, streams or ponds. Algal blooms are stimulated by phosphate enrichment.

ALPHA PARTICLE - A positively charged particle emitted by certain radioactive materials. It is the least penetrating of the three common types of radiation (alpha, beta and gamma) and usually not dangerous to plants, animals, or man.

AMBIENT AIR - Any unconfined portion of the atmosphere; the outside air.

ANADROMOUS - Type of fish that ascend rivers from the sea to spawn.

ANAEROBIC - Refers to life or processes that occur in the absence of oxygen.

ANTICOAGULANT - A chemical that intereferes with blood clotting, often used as a rodenticide.

ANTI-DEGRADATION CLAUSE - A provision in air quality and water quality laws that prohibits deterioration of air or water quality in areas where the pollution levels are presently below those allowed.

AQUIFER - An underground bed or stratum of earth, gravel, or porous stone that contains water.

AQUATIC PLANTS - Plants that grow in water, either floating on the surface, growing up from the bottom of the body of water, or growing under the surface of the water.

AREA SOURCE - In air pollution, any small individual fuel combustion source, including any transportation sources. This is a general definition; area source is legally and precisely defined in Federal regulations. (See POINT SOURCE.)

ASBESTOS - A mineral fiber with countless industrial uses; a hazardous air pollutant when inhaled.

A-SCALE SOUND LEVEL - The measurement of sound approximating the auditory sensitivity of the human ear. The A-Scale sound level is used to measure the relative noisiness or annoyance of common sounds.

ASSIMILATION - Conversion or incorporation of absorbed nutrients into protoplasm. Also refers to the ability of a body of water to purify itself of organic pollution.

ATMOSPHERE - The layer of air surrounding the earth.

ATOMIC PILE - A nuclear reactor.

ATTRACTANT - A chemical or agent that lures insects or other pests by olfactory stimulation.

ATTRITION - Wearing or grinding down by friction. One of the three basic contributing processes of air pollution; the others are vaporization and combustion.

AUDIOMETER - An instrument for measuring hearing sensitivity.
AUTOTROPHIC - Self-nourishing: denoting those organisms capable of constructing organic matter from inorganic substances.

B

BACKFILL - The material used to refill a ditch or other excavation, or the process of doing so.
BACKGROUND LEVEL - With respect to air pollution, amounts of pollutants present in the ambient air due to natural sources.
BACKGROUND RADIATION - Normal radiation present in the lower atmosphere from cosmic rays and from earth sources.
BACTERIA - Single-celled microorganisms that lack chlorophyll. Some bacteria are capable of causing human, animal, or plant diseases; others are essential in pollution control because they break down organic matter in the air and in the water.
BAFFLE - Any deflector device used to change the direction of flow or the velocity of water, sewage, or products of combustion such as fly ash or coarse particulate matter. Also used in deadening sound.
BAGHOUSE - An air pollution abatement device used to trap particu-lates by filtering gas streams through large fabric bags, usually made of glass fibers.
BALING - A means of reducing the volume of solid waste by compaction.
BALLISTIC SEPARATOR - A machine that separates inorganic from organic matter in a composting process.
BAND APPLICATION - With respect to pesticides, the application of the chemical over or next to each row of plants in a field.
BAR SCREEN - In waste water treatment, a screen that removes large floating and suspended solids.
BASAL APPLICATION - With respect to pesticides, the application of the pesticide formulation on stems or trunks of plants just above the soil line.
BASIN - (See RIVER BASIN.)
BENTHIC REGION - The bottom of a body of water. This region supports the benthos, a type of life that not only lives upon, but contributes to the character of the bottom.
BENTHOS - The plant and animal life whose habitat is the bottom of a sea, lake, or river.
BERYLLIUM - A metal that when airborne has adverse effects on human health, it has been declared a hazardous air pollutant. It is primarily discharged by operations such as machine shops, ceramic and propellant plants and foundries.
BETA PARTICLE - An elementary particle emitted by radioactive decay that may cause skin burns. It is easily stopped by a thin sheet of metal.
BIOASSAY - The employment of living organisms to determine the biological effect of some substance, factor, or condition.
BIOCHEMICAL OXYGEN DEMAND (BOD) - A measure of the amount of oxygen consumed in the biological processes that break down organic matter in water. Large amounts of organic waste use up large amounts of dissolved oxygen, thus the greater the degree of pollution, the greater the BOD.
BIODEGRADABLE - The process of decomposing quickly as a result of the action of microorganisms.
BIOLOGICAL CONTROL - A method of controlling pests by means of introduced or naturally occurring predatory organisms, sterilization, or the use of inhibiting hormones, etc. rather than by mechanical or chemical means.
BIOLOGICAL OXIDATION - The process by which bacterial and other microorganisms feed on complex organic materials and decompose them. Self-purification of waterways and activated

sludge and trickling filter waste water treatment processes depend on this principle. The process is also called biochemical oxidation.

BIOMONITORING - The use of living organisms to test the suitability of effluent for discharge into receiving waters and to test the quality of such waters downstream from a discharge.

BIOSPHERE - The portion of the earth and its atmosphere capable of supporting life.

BIOSTABILIZER - A machine used to convert solid waste into compost by grinding and aeration.

BIOTA - All the species of plants and animals occurring within a certain area.

BLOOM - A proliferation of living algae and/or other aquatic plants on the surface of lakes or ponds. Blooms are frequently stimulated by phosphate enrichment.

BOD - The amount of dissolved oxygen consumed in five days by biological processes breakdown of organic matter in an effluent. (See BIOCHEMICAL OXYGEN DEMAND.)

BOG - Wet, spongy land usually poorly drained, highly acid, and rich in plant residue.

BOOM - A floating device that is used to contain oil on a body of water.

BOTANICAL PESTICIDE - A plant-produced chemical used to control pests; for example, nicotine, strychnine, or orpyrethrun.

BRACKISH WATER - A mixture of fresh and salt water.

BREEDER - A nuclear reactor that produces more fuel than it consumes.

BROADCAST APPLICATION - With respect to pesticides, the application of a chemical over an entire field, lawn, or other area.

BURIAL GROUND (GRAVEYARD) - A place for burying unwanted radioactive materials to prevent radiation escape, the earth or water acting as a shield. Such materials must be placed in water-tight, noncorrodible containers so the radioactive material cannot leach out and invade underground water supplies.

<u>C</u>

CADMIUM - (See HEAVY METALS.)

CARBON DIOXIDE (CO_2) - A colorless, odorless, nonpoisonous gas that is a normal part of the ambient air. CO_2 is a product of fossil fuel combustion, and some researchers have theorized that excess CO_2 raises atmospheric temperatures.

CARBON MONOXIDE (CO) - A colorless, odorless, highly toxic gas that is a normal byproduct of incomplete fossil fuel combustion. CO, one of the major air pollutants, can be harmful in small amounts if breathed over a certain period of time.

CARCINOGENIC - Cancer producing.

CATALYTIC CONVERTER - An air pollution abatement device that removes organic contaminants by oxidizing them into carbon dioxide and water through chemical reaction. Can be used to reduce nitrogen oxide emissions from motor vehicles.

CAUSTIC SODA - Sodium hydroxide (NaOH), a strongly alkaline, caustic substance used as the cleaning agent in some detergents. CELLS - With respect to solid waste disposal, earthen compartments in which solid wastes are dumped, compacted, and covered over daily with layers of earth.

CENTRIFUGAL COLLECTOR - Any of several mechanical systems using centrifugal force to remove aerosols from a gas stream. CFS - Cubic feet per second, a measure of the amount of water passing a given point.

CHANNELIZATION - The straightening and deepening of streams to permit water to move faster, to reduce flooding, or to drain marshy acreage for farming. However, channelization reduces the organic waste assimilation capacity of the stream and may disturb fish breeding and destroy the stream's natural beauty.

CHEMICAL OXYGEN DEMAND (COD) - A measure of the amount of oxygen required to oxidize organic and oxidizable inorganic compounds in water. The COD test, like the BOD test, is used to determine the degree of pollution in an effluent.
CHEMOSTERILANT - A pesticide chemical that controls pests by destroying their ability to reproduce.
CHILLING EFFECT - The lowering of the earth's temperature due to the increase of atmospheric particulates that inhibit penetration of the sun's energy.
CHLORINATED HYDROCARBONS - A class of generally long-lasting, broad-spectrum insecticides of which the best known is DDT, first used for insect control during World War II. Other similar compounds include aldrin, dieldrin, heptachlor, chlordane, lindane, endrin, mirex, benzene hexachloride (BHC), and toxaphene. The qualities of persistence and effectivenss against a wide variety of insect pests were long regarded as highly desirable in agriculture, public health and home uses. But later research has revealed that these same qualities may represent a potential hazard through accumulation in the food chain and persistence in the environment.
CHLORINATION - The application of chlorine to drinking water, sewage or industrial waste for disinfection or oxidation of undesirable compounds.
CHLORINATOR - A device for adding a chlorine-containing gas or liquid to drinking or waste water.
CHLORINE-CONTACT CHAMBER - In a waste treatment plant, a chamber in which effluent is disinfected by chlorine before it is discharged to the receiving waters.
CHLOROSIS - Yellowing or whitening of normally green plant parts. It can be caused by disease organisms, lack of oxygen or nutrients in the soil or by various air pollutants.
CHROMIUM - (See HEAVY METALS.)
CHRONIC - Marked by long duration or frequent recurrence, as a disease.
CLARIFICATION - In waste water treatment, the removal of turbidity and suspended solids by settling, often aided by centrifugal action and chemically induced coagulation.
CLARIFIER - In waste water treatment, a settling tank which mechanically removes settleable solids from wastes.
COAGULATION - The clumping of particles in order to settle out impurities; often induced by chemicals such as lime or alum.
COASTAL ZONE - Coastal waters and adjacent lands that exert a measurable influence on the uses of the sea and its ecology.
COD - (See CHEMICAL OXYGEN DEMAND)
COEFFICIENT OF HAZE (COH) - A measurement of visibility interference in the atmosphere.
COFFIN - A thick-walled container (usually lead) used for transporting radioactive materials.
COH - (See COEFFICIENT OF HAZE)
COLIFORM INDEX - An index of the purity of water based on a count of its coliform bacteria.
COLIFORM ORGANISM - Any of a number of organisms common to the intestinal tract of man and animals whose presence in waste water is an indicator of pollution and of potentially dangerous bacterial contamination.
COMBINED SEWERS - A sewerage system that carries both sanitary sewage and storm water runoff. During dry weather, combined sewers carry all waste water to the treatment plant. During a storm, only part of the flow is intercepted because of plant overloading; the remainder goes untreated to the receiving stream.
COMBUSTION - Burning. Technically, a rapid oxidation accompanied by the release of energy in the form of heat and light. It is one of the three basic contributing factors causing air pollution; the others are attrition and vaporization.
COMMINUTION - Mechanical shredding or pulverizing of waste, a process that converts it into a homogeneous and more manageable material. Used in solid waste management and in the primary stage of waste water treatment.

COMMINUTOR - A device that grinds solids to make them easier to treat.
COMPACTION - Reducing the bulk of solid waste by rolling and tamping.
COMPOST - Relatively stable decomposed organic material.
COMPOSTING - A controlled process of degrading organic matter by microorganisms. (1) mechanical - a method in which the compost is continuously and mechanically mixed and aerated. (a) ventilated cell - compost is mixed and aerated by being dropped through a vertical series of ventilated cells. (3) windrow - an open-air method in which compostable material is placed in windrows, piles, or ventilated bins or pits and occasionally turned or mixed. The process may be anaerobic or aerobic.
CONTACT PESTICIDE - A chemical that kills pests on contact with the body, rather than by ingestion (stomach poison).
CONTRAILS - Long, narrow clouds caused by the disturbance of the atmosphere during passage of high-flying jets. Proliferation of contrails may cause changes in the weather.
COOLANT - A substance, usually liquid or gas, used for cooling any part of a reactor in which heat is generated, including the core, the reflector, shield, and other elements that may be heated by absorption of radiation.
COOLING TOWER - A device to remove excess heat from water used in industrial operations, notably in electric power generation.
CORE - The heart of a nuclear reactor where energy is released.
COVER MATERIAL - Soil that is used to cover compacted solid waste in a sanitary landfill.
CULTURAL EUTROPHICATION - Acceleration by man of the natural aging process of bodies of water.
CURIE - A measure of radiation.
CUTIE-PIE - A portable instrument equipped with a direct reading meter used to determine the level of radiation in an area.
CYCLONE COLLECTOR - A device used to collect large-size particulates from polluted air by centrifugal force.

_D_

DDT - The first of the modern chlorinated hydrocarbon insecticides whose chemical name is 1,1,1-tricholoro-2,2-bis (p-chloriphenyl)- ethane. It has a half-life of 15 years, and its residues can become concentrated in the fatty tissues of certain organisms, especially fish. Because of its persistence in the environment and its ability to accumulate and magnify in the food chain, EPA has banned the registration and interstate sale of DDT for nearly all uses in the United States effective December 31, 1972.
DECIBEL (dB) - A unit of sound measurement.
DECOMPOSITION - Reduction of the net energy level and change in chemical composition of organic matter because of the actions of aerobic or anaerobic microorganisms.
DERMAL TOXICITY - The ability of a pesticide chemical to poison an animal or human by skin absorption.
DESALINIZATION - Salt removal from sea or brackish water.
DESICCANT - A chemical that may be used to remove moisture from plants or insects causing them to wither and die.
DETERGENT - Synthetic washing agent that, like soap, lowers the surface tension of water, emulsifies oils and holds dirt in suspension. Environmentalists have criticized detergents because most contain large amounts of phosphorus-containing compounds that contribute to the eutrophication of waterways.

DIATOMACEOUS EARTH (DIATOMITE) - A fine siliceous material resembling chalk used in waste water treatment plants to filter sewage effluent to remove solids. May also be used as inactive ingredients in pesticide formulations applied as dust or powder.
DIFFUSED AIR - A type of sewage aeration. Air is pumped into the sewage through a perforated pipe.
DIGESTER - In a waste water treatment plant, a closed tank that decreases the volume of solids and stabilizes raw sludge by bacterial action.
DIGESTION - The biochemical decomposition of organic matter. Digestion of sewage sludge takes place in tanks where the sludge decomposes, resulting in partial gasification, liquefaction, and mineralization of pollutants.
DILUTION RATIO - The ratio of the volume of water of a stream to the volume of incoming waste. The capacity of a stream to assimilate waste is partially dependent upon the dilution ratio.
DISINFECTION - Effective killing by chemical or physical processes of all organisms capable of causing infectious diseases. Chlorination is the disinfection method commonly employed in sewage treatment processes.
DISPERSANT - A chemical agent used to break up concentrations of organic material. In cleaning oil spills, dispersants are used to disperse oil from the water surface.
DISSOLVED OXYGEN (DO) - The oxygen dissolved in water or sewage. Adequately dissolved oxygen is necessary for the life of fish and other aquatic organisms and for the prevention of offensive odors. Low dissolved oxygen concentrations generally are due to discharge of excessive organic solids having high BOD, the result of inadequate waste treatment.
DISSOLVED SOLIDS - The total amount of dissolved material, organic and inorganic, contained in water or wastes. Excessive dissolved solids make water unpalatable for drinking and unsuitable for industrial uses.
DISTILLATION - The removal of impurities from liquids by boiling. The steam, condensed back into liquid, is almost pure water; the pollutants remain in the concentrated residue.
DOSE - In radiology, the quantity of energy or radiation absorbed.
DOSIMETER (DOSEMETER) - An instrument used to measure the amount of radiation a person has received.
DREDGING - A method for deepening streams, swamps, or coastal waters by scraping and removing solids from the bottom. The resulting mud is usually deposited in marshes in a process called filling. Dredging and filling can disturb natural ecological cycles. For example, dredging can destroy oyster beds and other aquatic life; filling can destroy the feeding and breeding grounds for many fish species.
DRY LIMESTONE PROCESS - A method of controlling air pollution caused by sulfur oxides. The polluted gases are exposed to limestone which combines with oxides of sulfur to form manageable residues.
DUMP - A land site where solid waste is disposed of in a manner that does not protect the environment.
DUST - Fine-grain particulate matter that is capable of being suspended in air.
DUSTFALL JAR - An open-mouthed container used to collect large particles that fall out of the air. The particles are measured and analyzed.
DYSTROPHIC LAKES - Lakes between eutrophic and swamp stages of aging. Such lakes are shallow and have high humus content, high organic matter content, low nutrient availability, and high BOD.

E

ECOLOGICAL IMPACT - The total effect of an environmental change, either natural or man-made, on the ecology of the area.

ECOLOGY - The interrelationships of living things to one another and to their environment or the study of such interrelationships. ECONOMIC POISONS - Those chemicals used to control insects, rodents, plant diseases, weeds, and other pests, and also to defoliate economic crops such as cotton. ECOSPHERE - (See BIOSPHERE)

ECOSYSTEM - The interacting system of a biological community and its non-living environment.

EFFLUENT - A discharge of pollutants into the environment, partially or completely treated or in its natural state. Generally used in regard to discharges into waters.

ELECTRODIALYSIS - A process that uses electrical current and an arrangement of permeable membranes to separate soluble minerals from water. Often used to desalinize salt or brackish water.

ELECTROSTATIC PRECIPITATOR - An air pollution control device that removes particulate matter by imparting an electrical charge to particles in a gas stream for mechanical collection on an electrode.

EMERGENCY EPISODE - (See AIR POLLUTION EPISODE)

EMISSION - (See EFFLUENT) (Generally used in regard to discharges into air.)

EMISSION FACTOR - The average amount of a pollutant emitted from each type of polluting source in relation to a specific amount of material processed. For example, an emission factor for a blast furnace (used to make iron) would be a number of pounds of particulates per ton of raw materials.

EMISSION INVENTORY - A list of air pollutants emitted into a community's atmosphere, in amounts (usually tons) per day, by type of source. The emission inventory is basic to the establishment of emission standards.

EMISSION STANDARD - The maximum amount of a pollutant legally permitted to be discharged from a single source, either mobile or stationary.

ENRICHMENT - The addition of nitrogen, phosphorus, and carbon compounds or other nutrients into a lake or other waterway that greatly increases the growth potential for algae and other aquatic plants. Most frequently, enrichment results from the inflow of sewage effluent or from agricultural runoff.

ENVIRONMENT - The sum of all external conditions and influences affecting the life, development, and, ultimately, the survival of an organism.

ENVIRONMENTAL IMPACT STATEMENT - A document prepared by a Federal agency on the environmental impact of its proposals for legislation and other major actions significantly affecting the quality of the human environment. Environmental impact statements are used as tools for decision making and are required by the National Environmental Policy Act.

EPIDEMIOLOGY - The study of diseases as they affect populations.

EROSION - The wearing away of the land surface by wind or water. Erosion occurs naturally from weather or runoff but is often intensified by man's land-clearing practices.

ESTUARIES - Areas where the fresh water meets salt water. For example, bays, mouths of rivers, salt marshes, and lagoons. Estuaries are delicate ecosystems; they serve as nurseries, spawning and feeding grounds for a large group of marine life and provide shelter and food for birds and wildlife.

EUTROPHICATION - The normally slow aging process by which a lake evolves into a bog or marsh and ultimately assumes a completely terrestrial state and disappears. During eutrophication, the lake becomes so rich in nutritive compounds, especially nitrogen and phosphorus, that algae and other microscopic plant life becomes superabundant, thereby *choking* the lake and causing it eventually to dry up. Eutrophication may be accelerated by many human activities.

EUTROPHIC LAKES - Shallow lakes, weed-choked at the edges and very rich in nutrients. The water is characterized by large amounts of algae, low water transparency, low dissolved oxygen and high BOD.

EVAPORATION PONDS - Shallow, artificial ponds where sewage sludge is pumped, permitted to dry and either removed or buried by more sludge.

F

FABRIC FILTERS - A device for removing dust and particulate matter from industrial emissions much like a home vacuum cleaner bag. The most common use of fabric filters is the baghouse.

FECAL COLIFORM BACTERIA - A group of organisms common to the intestinal tracts of man and of animals. The presence of fecal coliform bacteria in water is an indicator of pollution and of potentially dangerous bacterial contamination.

FEEDLOT - A relatively small, confined land area for raising cattle. Although an economical method of fattening beef, feedlots concentrate a large amount of animal wastes in a small area. This excrement cannot be handled by the soil as it could be if the cattle were scattered on open range. In addition, runoff from feedlots contributes excessive quantities of nitrogen, phosphorus, and potassium to nearby waterways, thus contributing to eutrophication.

FEN - A low-lying land area partly covered by water.

FILLING - The process of depositing dirt and mud in marshy areas to create more land for real estate development. Filling can disturb natural ecological cycles. (See DREDGING)

FILM BADGE - A piece of masked photographic film worn like a badge by nuclear workers to monitor an exposure to radiation. Nuclear radiation darkens the film.

FILTRATION - In waste water treatment, the mechanical process that removes particulate matter by separating water from solid material usually by passing it through sand.

FLOC - A clump of solids formed in sewage by biological or chemical action.

FLOCCULATION - In waste water treatment, the process of separating suspended solids by chemical creation of clumps or floes.

FLOWMETER - In waste water treatment, a meter that indicates the rate at which waste water flows through the plant.

FLUE GAS - A mixture of gases resulting from combustion and emerging from a chimney. Flue gas includes nitrogen oxides, carbon oxides, water vapor, and often sulfur oxides or particulates.

FLUORIDES - Gaseous, solid or dissolved compounds containing fluorine, emitted into the air or water from a number of industrial processes. Fluorides in the air are a cause of vegetation damage and, indirectly, of livestock damage.

FLUME - A channel, either natural or manmade, which carries water.

FLY ASH - All solids, including ash, charred paper, cinders, dust, soot or other partially incinerated matter, that are carried in a gas stream.

FOG - Liquid particles formed by condensation of vaporized liquids.

FOGGING - The application of a pesticide by rapidly heating the liquid chemical, thus forming very fine droplets with the appearance of smoke. Fogging is often used to destroy mosquitoes and blackflies.

FOOD WASTE - Animal and vegetable waste resulting from the handling, storage, sale, preparation, cooking and serving of foods; commonly called garbage.

FOSSIL FUELS - Coal, oil, and natural gas; so-called because they are derived from the remains of ancient plant and animal life.

FUME - Tiny solid particles commonly formed by the condensation of vapors of solid matter.

FUMIGANT - A pesticide that is burned or evaporated to form a gas or vapor that destroys pests. Fumigants are often used in buildings or greenhouses.

FUNGI - Small, often microscopic plants without chlorophyll. Some fungi infect and cause disease in plants or animals; other fungi are useful in stabilizing sewage or in breaking down wastes for compost.

FUNGICIDE - A pesticide chemical that kills fungi or prevents them from causing diseases, usually on plants of economic importance. (See PESTICIDE)

G

GAME FISH - Those species of fish sought by sports fishermen; for example, salmon, trout, black bass, striped bass, etc. Game fish are usually more sensitive to environmental changes and water quality degradation than *rough* fish.

GAMMA RAY - Waves of radiant nuclear energy. Gamma rays are the most penetrating of the three types of radiation and are best stopped by dense materials such as lead.

GARBAGE - (See FOOD WASTE)

GARBAGE GRINDING - A method of grinding food waste by a household disposal, for example, and washing it into the sewer system. Ground garbage then must be disposed of as sewage sludge.

GEIGER COUNTER - An electrical device that detects the presence of radioactivity.

GENERATOR - A device that converts mechanical energy into electrical energy.

GERMICIDE - A chemical or agent that kills microorganisms such as bacteria and prevents them from causing disease. Such compounds must be registered as pesticides with EPA.

GRAIN - A unit of weight equivalent to 65 milligrams or 2/1,000 of an ounce.

GRAIN LOADING - The rate of emission of particulate matter from a polluting source. Measurement is made in grains of particulate matter per cubic foot of gas emitted.

GREEN BELTS - Certain areas restricted from being used for buildings and houses; they often serve as separating buffers between pollution sources and concentrations of population.

GREENHOUSE EFFECT - The heating effect of the atmosphere upon the earth. Light waves from the sun pass through the air and are absorbed by the earth. The earth then reradiates this energy as heat waves that are absorbed by the air, specifically by carbon dioxide. The air thus behaves like glass in a greenhouse, allowing the passage of light but not of heat. Thus, many scientists theorize that an increase in the atmospheric concentration of CO_2 can eventually cause an increase in the earth's surface temperature.

GROUND COVER - Grasses or other plants grown to keep soil from being blown or washed away.

GROUNDWATER - The supply of freshwater under the earth's surface in an aquifer or soil that forms the natural reservoir for man's use.

GROUNDWATER RUNOFF - Groundwater that is discharged into a stream channel as spring or seepage water.

H

HABITAT - The sum total of environmental conditions of a specific place that is occupied by an organism, a population or a community.

HALF-LIFE - The time it takes certain materials, such as persistent pesticides or radioactive isotopes, to lose half their strength. For example, the half-life of DDT is 15 years; the half-life of radium is 1,580 years.

HAMMERMILL - A broad category of high speed equipment that uses pivoted or fixed hammers or cutters to crush, grind, chip, or shred solid wastes.

HARD WATER - Water containing dissolved minerals such as calcium, iron, and magnesium. The most notable characteristic of hard water is its inability to lather soap. Some pesticide chemicals will curdle or settle out when added to hard water.

HAZARDOUS AIR POLLUTANT - According to law, a pollutant to which no ambient air quality standard is applicable and that may cause or contribute to an increase in mortality or in serious illness. For example, asbestos, beryllium, and mercury have been declared hazardous air pollutants.

HEAT ISLAND EFFECT - An air circulation problem peculiar to cities. Tall buildings, heat from pavements, and concentrations of pollutants create a haze dome that prevents rising hot air from being cooled at its normal rate. A self-contained circulation system is put in motion that can be broken by relatively strong winds. If such winds are absent, the heat island can trap high concentrations of pollutants and present a serious health problem.

HEATING SYSTEM - The coldest months of the year when pollution emissions are higher in some areas because of increased fossil-fuel consumption.

HEAVY METALS - Metallic elements with high molecular weights, generally toxic in low concentrations to plant and animal life. Such metals are often residual in the environment and exhibit biological accumulation. Examples include mercury, chromium, calcium, arsenic, and lead.

HERBICIDE - A pesticide chemical used to destroy or control the growth of weeds, bush, and other undesirable plants. (See PESTICIDE)

HERBIVORE - An organism that feeds on vegetation.

HETEROTROPHIC ORGANISM - Organisms dependent on organic matter for food.

HIGH DENSITY POLYETHYLENE - A material often used in the manufacture of plastic bottles that produces toxic fumes if incinerated.

HI-VOLUME SAMPLER - A device used in the measurement and analysis of suspended particulate pollution. Also called a Hi-Vol.

HOT - A colloquial term meaning highly radioactive.

HUMUS - Decomposed organic material.

HYDROCARBONS - A vast family of compounds containing carbon and hydrogen in various combinations, found especially in fossil fuels. Some hydrocarbons are major air pollutants, some may be carcinogenic and others contribute to photochemical smog.

HYDROGEN SULFIDE (H_2S) - A malodorous gas made up of hydrogen and sulfur with the characteristic odor of rotten eggs. It is emitted in the natural decomposition of organic matter and is also the natural accompaniment of advanced stages of eutrophication. H_2S is also a byproduct of refinery activity and the combustion of oil during power plant operations. In heavy concentrations, it can cause illness.

HYDROLOGY - The science dealing with the properties, distribution, and circulation of water and snow.

I

IMPEDANCE - The rate at which a substance can absorb and transmit sound.

IMPLEMENTATION PLAN - A document of the steps to be taken to ensure attainment of environmental quality standards within a specified time period. Implementation plans are required by various laws.

IMPOUNDMENT - A body of water, such as a pond, confined by a dam, dike, floodgate, or other barrier.

INCINERATION - The controlled process by which solid, liquid, or gaseous combustible wastes are burned and changed into gases; the residue produced contains little or no combustible material.

INCINERATOR - An engineered apparatus used to burn waste substances and in which all the combustion factors - temperature, retention time, turbulence, and combustion air - can be controlled.

INERT GAS - A gas that does not react with other substances under ordinary conditions.

INERTIAL SEPARATOR - An air pollution control device that uses the principle of inertia to remove particulate matter from a stream of air or gas.

INFILTRATION - The flow of a fluid into a substance through pores or small openings. Commonly used in hydrology to denote the flow of water into soil material.

INOCULUM - Material such as bacteria placed in compost or other medium to initiate biological action.

INTEGRATED PEST CONTROL - A system of managing pests by using biological, cultural, and chemical means.

INTERCEPTOR SEWERS - Sewers used to collect the flows from main and trunk sewers and carry them to a central point for treatment and discharge. In a combined sewer system, where street runoff from rains is allowed to enter the system along with sewage, interceptor sewers allow some of the sewage to flow untreated directly into the receiving stream, to prevent the plant from being overloaded.

INTERSTATE CARRIER WATER SUPPLY - A water supply whose water may be used for drinking or cooking purposes aboard common carriers (planes, trains, buses, and ships) operating interstate. Interstate carrier water supplies are regulated by the Federal government.

INTERSTATE WATERS - According to law, waters defined as (1) rivers, lakes and other waters that flow across or form a part of state or international boundaries; (2) waters of the Great Lakes; (3) coastal waters - whose scope has been defined to include ocean waters seaward to the territorial limits and waters along the coastline (including inland streams) influenced by the tide.

INVERSION - An atmospheric condition where a layer of cool air is trapped by a layer of warm air so that it cannot rise. Inversions spread polluted air horizontally rather than vertically so that contaminating substances cannot be widely dispersed. An inversion of several days can cause an air pollution episode.

IONIZATION CHAMBER - A device roughly similar to a geiger counter that reveals the presence of ionizing radiation.

ISOTOPE - A variation of an element having the same atomic number as the element itself, but having a different atomic weight because of a different number of neutrons. Different isotopes of the same element have different radioactive behavior.

L

LAGOON - In waste water treatment, a shallow pond usually man-made where sunlight, bacterial action, and oxygen interact to restore waste water to a reasonable state of purity.

LATERAL SEWERS - Pipes running underneath city streets that collect sewage from homes or businesses.

LC_{50} - Median lethal concentration, a standard measure of toxicity.

LC_{50} indicates the concentration of a substance that will kill 50 percent of a group of experimental insects or animals.

LEACHATE - Liquid that has percolated through solid waste or other mediums and has extracted dissolved or suspended materials from it.

LEACHING - The process by which soluble materials in the soil, such as nutrients, pesticide chemicals or contaminants, are washed into a lower layer of soil or are dissolved and carried away by water.

LEAD - A heavy metal that may be hazardous to human health if breathed or ingested.

LIFE CYCLE - The phases, changes or stages an organism passes through during its lifetime.

LIFT - In a sanitary landfill, a compacted layer of solid waste and the top layer of cover material.

LIMNOLOGY - The study of the physical, chemical, meteorological, and biological aspects of fresh waters.

M

MARSH - A low-lying tract of soft, wet land that provides an important ecosystem for a variety of plant and animal life but often is destroyed by dredging and filling.

MASKING - Covering over of one sound or element by another. Quantitatively, masking is the amount of audibility threshold of one sound is raised by the presence of a second masking sound. Also used in regard to odors.

MECHANICAL TURBULENCE - The erratic movement of air caused by local obstructions, such as buildings.

MERCURY - A heavy metal, highly toxic if breathed or ingested. Mercury is residual in the environment, showing biological accumulation in all aquatic organisms, especially fish and shellfish. Chronic exposure to airborne mercury can have serious effect on the central nervous system.

METHANE - Colorless, nonpoisonous, and flammable gaseous hydrocarbon. Methane (CA) is emitted by marshes and by dumps undergoing anaerobic decomposition.

MOD - Millions of gallons per day. Mgd is commonly used to express rate of flow.

MICROBES - Minute plant or animal life. Some disease-causing microbes exist in sewage.

MIST - Liquid particles in air formed by condensation of vaporized liquids. Mist particles vary from 500 to 40 microns in size. By comparison, fog particles are smaller than 40 microns in size. MIXED LIQUOR - A mixture of activated sludge and water containing organic matter undergoing activated sludge treatment in the aeration tank.

MOBILE SOURCE - A moving source of air pollution such as an automobile.

MONITORING - Periodic or continuous determination of the amount of pollutants or radioactive contamination present in the environment.

MUCK SOILS - Soils made from decaying plant materials.

MULCH - A layer of wood chips, dry leaves, straw, hay, plastic strips or other material placed on the soil around plants to retain moisture, to prevent weeds from growing, and to enrich soil.

N

NATURAL GAS - A fuel gas occurring naturally in certain geologic formation. Natural gas is usually a combustible mixture of methane and hydrocarbons.

NATURAL SELECTION - The natural process by which the organisms best adapted to their environment survive and those less well adapted are eliminated.

NECROSIS - Death of plant cells resulting in a discolored, sunken area or death of the entire plant.

NITRIC OXIDE (NO) - A gas formed in great part from atmospheric nitrogen and oxygen when combustion takes place under high temperature and high pressure, as in internal combustion engines. NO is not itself a pollutant; however, in the ambient air, it converts to nitrogen dioxide, a major contributor to photochemical smog.

NITROGEN DIOXIDE (NO_2) - A compound produced by the oxidation of nitric oxide in the atmosphere; a major contributor to photochemical smog.

NITROGENOUS WASTES - Wastes of animal or plant origin that contain a significant concentration of nitrogen.

NO - A notation meaning oxides of nitrogen. (See NITRIC OXIDE)

NOISE - Any undesired audible signal. Thus, in acoustics, noise is any undesired sound.

NTA - Nitrilotriacetic acid, a compound once used to replace phosphates in detergents.

NUCLEAR POWER PLANT - Any device, machine, or assembly that converts nuclear energy into some form of useful power, such as mechanical or electrical power. In a nuclear electric power plant, heat produced by a reactor is generally used to make steam to drive a turbine that in turn drives an electric generator.

NUTRIENTS - Elements or compounds essential as raw materials for organism growth and development; for example, carbon, oxygen, nitrogen, and phosphorus.

O

OIL SPILL - The accidental discharge of oil into oceans, bays or inland waterways. Methods of oil spill control include chemical dispersion, combustion, mechanical containment, and absorption.

OLIGOTROPHIC LAKES - Deep lakes that have a low supply of nutrients and thus contain little organic matter. Such lakes are characterized by high water transparency and high dissolved oxygen. OPACITY - Degree of obscuration of light. For example, a window has zero opacity; a wall is 100 percent opaque. The Ringelmann system of evaluating smoke density is based on opacity. OPEN BURNING - Uncontrolled burning of wastes in an open dump.

OPEN DUMP - (See DUMP)

ORGANIC - Referring to or derived from living organisms. In chemistry, any compound containing carbon.

ORGANISM - Any living human, plant or animal.

ORGANOPHOSPHATES - A group of pesticide chemicals containing phosphorus, such as malathion and parathion, intended to control insects. These compounds are short-lived and, therefore, do not normally contaminate the environment. However, some organophosphates, such as parathion, are extremely toxic when initially applied and exposure to them can interfere with the normal processes of the nervous system, causing convulsions and eventually death. Malathion, on the other hand, is low in toxicity and relatively safe for humans and animals. It is a common ingredient in household insecticide products.

OUTFALL - The mouth of a sewer, drain or conduit where an effluent is discharged into the receiving waters.

OVERFIRE AIR - Air forced into the top of an incinerator to fan the flame.

OXIDANT - Any oxygen containing substance that reacts chemically in the air to produce new substances. Oxidants are the primary contributors to photochemical smog.

OXIDATION - A chemical reaction in which oxygen unites or combines with other elements. Organic matter is oxidized by the action of aerobic bacteria; thus, oxidation is used in waste water treatment to break down organic wastes.

OXIDATION POND - A man-made lake or pond in which organic wastes are reduced by bacterial action. Often oxygen is bubbled through the pond to speed the process.

OZONE (O_2) - A pungent, colorless, toxic gas. Ozone is one component of photochemical smog and is considered a major air pollutant.

P

PACKAGE PLANT - A prefabricated or prebuilt waste water treatment plant.

PACKED TOWER - An air pollution control device in which polluted air is forced upward through a tower packed with crushed rock or wood chips while the liquid is sprayed downward on the packing material. The pollutants in the air stream either dissolve or chemically react with the liquid.

PAN - Peroxyacetyl nitrate, a pollutant created by the action of sunlight on hydrocarbons and nitrogen oxides in the air. PANS are an integral part of photochemical smog.

PARTICULATES - Finely divided solid or liquid particles in the air or in air emission. Particulates include dust, smoke, fumes, mist, spray, and fog.

PARTICULATE LOADING - The introduction of particulates into the ambient air.

PATHOGENIC - Causing or capable of causing disease.

PCBs - Polychlorinated biphenyls, a group of organic compounds used in the manufacture of plastics. In the environment, PCBs exhibit many of the same characteristics as DDT and may, therefore, be confused with that pesticide. PCBs are highly toxic to aquatic life; they persist in the environment for long periods of time, and they are biologically accumulative.

PEAT - Partially decomposed organic material.

PERCOLATION - Downward flow or infiltration of water through the pores or spaces of a rock or soil.

PERSISTENT PESTICIDES - Pesticides that will be present in the environment for longer than one growing season or one year after application.

PESTICIDE - An agent used to control pests. This includes insecticides for use against harmful insects, herbicides for weed control, fungicides for control of plant diseases, rodenticides for killing rats, mice, etc., and germicides used in disinfectant products, algaecides, slimicides, etc. Some pesticides can contaminate water, air or soil and accumulate in man, animals, and the environment, particularly if they are misused. Certain of these chemicals have been shown to interfere with the reproductive processes of predatory birds and possibly other animals.

PESTICIDE TOLERANCE - A scientifically and legally established limit for the amount of chemical residue that can be permitted to remain in or on a harvested food or feed crop as a result of the application of a chemical for pest-control purposes. Such tolerances or safety levels, established federally by EPA, are set well below the point at which residues might be harmful to consumers.

pH - A measure of the acidity or alkalinity of a material, liquid, or solid. pH is represented on a scale of 0 to 14, with 7 representing a neutral state, 0 representing the most acid and 14, the most alkaline.

PHENOLS - A group of organic compounds that in very low concentrations produce a taste and odor problem in water. In higher concentrations, they are toxic to aquatic life. Phenols are byproducts of petroleum refining, tanning and textile, dye and resin manufacture.

PHOSPHORUS - An element that, while essential to life, contributes to the eutrophication of lakes and other bodies of water.

PHOTOCHEMICAL OXIDANTS - Secondary pollutants formed by the action of nitrogen and hydrocarbons in the air; they are the primary contributors to photochemical smog.

PHOTOCHEMICAL SMOG - Air pollution associated with oxidants rather than with sulfur oxides, particulates, etc. Produces necrosis, chlorosis, and growth alterations in plants and is an eye and respiratory irritant in humans.

PHYTOPLANKTON - The plant portion of plankton.

PHYTOTOXIC - Injurious to plants.

PIG - A container usually made of lead used to ship or store radioactive materials.

PILE - A nuclear reactor.

PLANKTON - The floating or weakly swimming plant and animal life in a body of water, often microscopic in size.

PLUME - The visible emission from a flue or chimney.

POINT SOURCE - In air pollution, a stationary source of a large individual emission, generally of an industrial nature. This is a general definition; point source is legally and precisely defined in Federal regulations. (See AREA SOURCE)

POLLEN - A fine dust produced by plants; a natural or background air pollutant.

POLLUTANT - Any introduced gas, liquid or solid that makes a resource unfit for a specific purpose.

POLLUTION - The presence of matter or energy whose nature, location, or quantity produces undesired environmental effects.

POLYELECTROLYTES - Synthetic chemicals used to speed flocculation of solids in sewage.

POTABLE WATER - Water suitable for drinking or cooking purposes from both health and aesthetic considerations.

PPM - Parts per million. The unit commonly used to represent the degree of pollutant concentration where the concentrations are small. Larger concentrations are given in percentages. Thus, BOD is represented in ppm, while suspended solids in water are expressed in percentages. In air, ppm is usually a volume/volume ratio; in water, a weight/volume ratio.

PRECIPITATE - A solid that separates from a solution because of some chemical or physical change or the formation of such a solid.

PRECIPITATORS - In pollution control work, any of a number of air pollution control devices usually using mechanical/electrical means to collect particulates from an emission.

PRETREATMENT - In waste water treatment, any process used to reduce pollution load before the waste water is introduced into a main sewer system or delivered to a treatment plant for substantial reduction of the pollution load.

PRIMARY TREATMENT - The first stage in waste water treatment in which substantially all floating or settleable solids are mechanically removed by screening and sedimentation.

PROCESS WEIGHT - The total weight of all materials, including fuels, introduced into a manufacturing process. The process weight is used to calculate the allowable rate of emission of pollutant matter from the process.

PULVERIZATION - The crushing or grinding of material into small pieces.

PUMPING STATION - A station at which sewage is pumped to a higher level. In most sewer systems, pumping is unnecessary; waste water flows by gravity to the treatment plant.

PUTRESCIBLE - Capable of being decomposed by microorganisms with sufficient rapidity to cause nuisances from odors, gases, etc. For example, kitchen wastes or dead animals.

Q

QUENCH TANK - A water-filled tank used to cool incinerator residues.

R

RAD - A unit of measurement of any kind of radiation absorbed by man.

RADIATION - The emission of fast atomic particles or rays by the nucleus of an atom. Some elements are naturally radioactive while others become radioactive after bombardment with neutrons or other particles. The three major forms of radiation are alpha, beta, and gamma.

RADIATION STANDARDS - Regulations that include exposure standards, permissible concentrations and regulations for transportation.

RADIOBIOLOGY - The study of the principles, mechanisms, and effects of radiation on living matter.

RADIOECOLOGY - The study of the effects of radiation on species of plants and animals in natural communities.

RADIOISOTOPES - Radioactive isotopes. Radioisotopes, such as cobalt-60, are used in the treatment of disease.

RASP - A device used to grate solid waste into a more manageable material, ridding it of much of its odor.

RAW SEWAGE - Untreated domestic or commercial waste water.

RECEIVING WATERS - Rivers, lakes, oceans, or other bodies that receive treated or untreated waste waters.

RECYCLING - The process by which waste materials are transformed into new products in such a manner that the original products may lose their identity.

RED TIDE - A proliferation or bloom of a certain type of plankton with red-to-orange coloration, that often causes massive fish kills. Though they are a natural phenomenon, blooms are believed to be stimulated by phosphorus and other nutrients discharged into waterways by man.

REFUSE - (See SOLID WASTE)
REFUSE RECLAMATION - The process of converting solid waste to saleable products. For example, the composting of organic solid waste yields a saleable soil conditioner.
REM - A measurement of radiation dose to the internal tissues of man.
REP - A unit of measurement of any kind of radiation absorbed by man.
RESERVOIR - A pond, lake, tank, or basin, natural or man-made, used for the storage, regulation, and control of water.
RESOURCE RECOVERY - The process of obtaining materials or energy, particularly from solid waste.
REVERBERATION - The persistence of sound in an enclosed space after the sound source has stopped.
RINGELMANN CHART - A series of illustrations ranging from light grey to black used to measure the opacity of smoke emitted from stacks and other sources. The shades of grey simulate various moke densities and are assigned numbers ranging from one to five. Ringelmann No. 1 is equivalent to 20 percent dense; No. 5 is 100 percent dense. Ringelmann charts are used in the setting and enforcement of emission standards.
RIPARIAN RIGHTS - Rights of a land owner to the water on or bordering his property, including the right to prevent diversion or misuse of upstream water.
RIVER BASIN - The total area drained by a river and its tributaries.
RODENTICIDE - A chemical or agent used to destroy or prevent damage by rats or other rodent pests. (See PESTICIDE)
ROUGH FISH - Those fish species considered to be of poor fighting quality when taken on tackle or of poor eating quality; for example, gar, suckers, etc. Most rough fish are more tolerant of widely changing environmental conditions than are game fish.
RUBBISH - A general term for solid waste, excluding food waste and ashes, taken from residences, commercial establishments, and institutions.
RUNOFF - The portion of rainfall, melted snow, or irrigation water that flows across ground surface and eventually is returned to streams. Runoff can pick up pollutants from the air or the land and carry them to the receiving waters.

<u>S</u>

SALINITY - The degree of salt in water.
SALT WATER INTRUSION - The invasion of salt water into a body of fresh water, occurring in either surface or groundwater bodies. When this invasion is caused by oceanic waters, it is called sea water intrusion.
SALVAGE - The utilization of waste materials.
SANITATION - The control of all the factors in man's physical environment that exercise or can exercise a deleterious effect on his physical development, health, and survival.
SANITARY LANDFILL - A site for solid waste disposal using sanitary landfilling techniques.
SANITARY LANDFILLING - An engineered method of solid waste disposal on land in a manner that protects the environment; waste is spread in thin layers, compacted to the smallest practical volume and covered with soil at the end of each working day. SANITARY SEWERS - Sewers that carry only domestic or commercial sewage. Storm water runoff is carried in a separate system. (See SEWER)
SCRAP - Discarded or rejected materials that result from manufacturing or fabricating operations and are suitable for reprocessing.

SCREENING - The removal of relatively coarse floating and suspended solids by straining through racks or screens.

SCRUBBER - An air pollution control device that uses a liquid spray to remove pollutants from a gas stream by absorption or chemical reaction. Scrubbers also reduce the temperature of the emission.

SECONDARY TREATMENT - Waste water treatment, beyond the primary stage, in which bacteria consume the organic parts of the wastes. This biochemical action is accomplished by use of trickling filters or the activated sludge process. Effective secondary treatment removes virtually all floating and settleable solids and approximately 90 percent of both BOD_3 and suspended solids. Customarily, disinfection by chlorination is the final stage of the secondary treatment process.

SEDIMENTATION - In waste water treatment, the settling out of solids by gravity.

SEDIMENTATION TANKS - In waste water treatment, tanks where the solids are allowed to settle or to float as scum. Scum is skimmed off; settled solids are pumped to incinerators, digesters, filters, or other means of disposal.

SEEPAGE - Water that flows through the soil.

SELECTIVE HERBICIDE - A pesticide intended to kill only certain types of plants, especially broad-leafed weeds, and not harm other plants such as farm crops or lawn grasses. The leading herbicide in the United States is 2,4-D. A related but stronger chemical used mostly for brush control on range, pasture, and forest lands and on utility or highway rights-of-way is 2,4,5-T. Uses of the latter chemical have been somewhat restricted because of laboratory evidence that it or a dioxin contaminant in 2,4,5-T can cause birth defects in test animals.

SENESCENCE - The process of growing old. Sometimes used to refer to lakes nearing extinction.

SEPTIC TANK - An underground tank used for the deposition of domestic wastes. Bacteria in the wastes decompose the organic matter, and the sludge settles to the bottom. The effluent flows through drains into the ground. Sludge is pumped out at regular intervals.

SETTLEABLE SOLIDS - Bits of debris and fine matter heavy enough to settle out of waste water.

SETTLING CHAMBER - In air pollution control, a low-cost device used to reduce the velocity of flue gases usually by means of baffles, promoting the settling of fly ash.

SETTLING TANK - In waste water treatment, a tank or basin in which settleable solids are removed by gravity.

SEWAGE - The total of organic waste and waste water generated by residential and commercial establishments.

SEWAGE LAGOON - (See LAGOON)

SEWER - Any pipe or conduit used to collect and carry away sewage or storm water runoff from the generating source to treatment plants or receiving streams. A sewer that conveys household and commercial sewage is called a sanitary sewer. If it transports runoff from rain or snow, it is called a storm sewer. Often storm water runoff and sewage are transported in the same system or combined sewers.

SEWERAGE - The entire system of sewage collection, treatment, and disposal. Also applies to all effluent carried by sewers, whether it is sanitary sewage, industrial wastes, or storm water runoff.

SHIELD - A wall that protects workers from harmful radiation released by radioactive materials.

SILT - Finely divided particles of soil or rock. Often carried in cloudy suspension in water and eventually deposited as sediment.

SINKING - A method of controlling oil spills that employs an agent to entrap oil droplets and sink them to the bottom of the body of water. The oil and sinking agent are eventually biologically degraded.

SKIMMING - The mechanical removal of oil or scum from the surface of water.
SLUDGE - The construction of solids removed from sewage during waste water treatment. Sludge disposal is then handled by incineration, dumping, or burial.
SMOG - Generally used as an equivalent of air pollution, particularly associated with oxidants.
SMOKE - Solid particles generated as a result of the incomplete combustion of materials containing carbon.
SO_x - A symbol meaning oxides of sulfur.
SOFT DETERGENTS - Biodegradable detergents.
SOIL CONDITIONER - A biologically stable organic material such as humus or compost that makes soil more amenable to the passage of water and to the distribution of fertilizing material, providing a better medium for necessary soil bacteria growth.
SOLID WASTE - Useless, unwanted or discarded material with insufficient liquid content to be free flowing. Also see WASTE. (1)

(1) Agricultural - solid waste that results from the raising and slaughtering of animals, and the processing of animal products and orchard and field crops.

(2) Commercial - waste generated by stores, offices, and other activities that do not actually turn out a product.

(3) Industrial - waste that results from industrial processes and manufacturing.

(4) Institutional - waste originating from educational, health care, and research facilities.

(5) Municipal - residential and commercial solid waste generated within a community.

(6) Pesticide - the residue from the manufacturing, handling or use of chemicals intended for killing plant and animal pests.

(7) Residential - waste that normally originates in a residential environment. Sometimes called domestic solid waste.

SOLID WASTE DISPOSAL - The ultimate disposition of refuse that cannot be salvaged or recycled.
SOLID WASTE MANAGEMENT - The purposeful, systematic control of the generation, storage, collection, transport, separation, processing, recycling, recovery, and disposal of solid wastes.
SONIC BOOM - The tremendous booming sound produced as a vehicle, usually a supersonic jet airplane, exceeds the speed of sound, and the shock wave reaches the ground.
SOOT - Agglomerations of tar-impregnated carbon particles that form when carbonaceous material does not undergo complete combustion.
SORPTION - A term including both adsorption and absorption. Sorption is basic to many processes used to remove gaseous and particulate pollutants from an emission and to clean up oil spills.
SPOIL - Dirt or rock that has been removed from its original location, specifically materials that have been dredged from the bottom of waterways.
STABILIZATION - The process of converting active organic matter in sewage sludge or solid wastes into inert, harmless material.
STABILIZATION PONDS - (See LAGOON, OXIDATION POND)
STABLE AIR - An air mass that remains in the same position rather than moving in its normal horizontal and vertical directions. Stable air does not disperse pollutants and can lead to high build-ups of air pollution.
STACK - A smokestack; a vertical pipe or flue designed to exhaust gases and suspended particulate matter.
STACK EFFECT - The upward movement of hot gases in a stack due to the temperature difference between the gases and the atmosphere.
STAGNATION - Lack of wind in an air mass or lack of motion in water. Both cases tend to entrap and concentrate pollutants.

STATIONARY SOURCE - A pollution emitter that is fixed rather than moving as an automobile.
STORM SEWER - A conduit that collects and transports rain and snow runoff back to the ground water. In a separate sewerage system, storm sewers are entirely separate from those carrying domestic and commercial waste water.
STRATIFICATION - Separating into layers.
STRIP MINING - A process in which rock and top soil strat overlying ore or fuel deposits are scraped away by mechanical shovels. Also known as surface mining.
SULFUR DIOXIDE
(SO_2) - A heavy, pungent, colorless gas formed primarily by the combustion of fossil fuels. SO_2 damages the respiratory tract as well as vegetation and materials and is considered a major air pollutant.
SUMP - A depression or tank that serves as a drain or receptacle for liquids for salvage or disposal.
SURFACTANT - An agent used in detergents to cause lathering. Composed of several phosphate compounds, surfactants are a source of external enrichment thought to speed the eutrophication of our lakes.
SURVEILLANCE SYSTEM - A monitoring system to determine environmental quality. Surveillance systems should be established to monitor all aspects of progress toward attainment of environmental standards and to identify potential episodes of high pollutant concentrations in time to take preventive action.
SUSPENDED SOLIDS (SS) - Small particles of solid pollutants in sewage that contribute to turbidity and that resist separation by conventional means. The examination of suspended solids and the BOD test constitute the two main determinations for water quality performed at waste water treatment facilities.
SYNERGISM - The cooperative action of separate substances so that the total effect is greater than the sum of the effects of the substances acting independently.
SYSTEMIC PESTICIDE - A pesticide chemical that is carried to other parts of a plant or animal after it is injected or taken up from the soil or body surface.

T

TAILINGS - Second grade or waste material derived when raw material is screened or processed.
TERTIARY TREATMENT - Waste water treatment beyond the secondary or biological stage that includes removal of nutrients such as phosphorus and nitrogen and a high percentage of suspended solids. Tertiary treatment, also known as advanced waste treatment, produces a high quality effluent.
THERMAL POLLUTION - Degradation of water quality by the introduction of the heated effluent. Primarily a result of the discharge of cooling waters from industrial processes, particularly from electrical power generation. Even small deviations from normal water temperatures can affect aquatic life. Thermal pollution usually can be controlled by cooling towers.
THRESHOLD DOSE - The minimum dose of given substance necessary to produce a measurable physiological or psychological effect.
TOLERANCE - The relative capability of an organism to endure an unfavorable environmental factor. The amount of a chemical considered safe on any food to be eaten by man or animals. (See PESTICIDE TOLERANCE)
TOPOGRAPHY - The configuration of a surface area including its relief or relative elevations and the position of its natural and man-made features.

TOXICANT - A substance that kills or injures an organism through its chemical or physical action or by altering its environment; for example, cyanides, phenols, pesticides or heavy metals. Especially used for insect control.
TOXICITY - The quality or degree of being poisonous or harmful to plant or animal life.
TRICKLING FILTER - A device for the biological or secondary treatment of waste water consisting of a bed of rocks or stones that support bacterial growth. Sewage is trickled over the bed, enabling the bacteria to break down organic wastes.
TROPOSPHERE - The layer of the atmosphere extending seven to ten miles above the earth. Vital to life on earth, it contains clouds and moisture that reach earth as rain or snow.
TURBIDIMETER - A device used to measure the amount of suspended solids in a liquid.
TURBIDITY - A thick, hazy condition of air due to the presence of particulates or other pollutants, or the similar cloudy condition in water due to the suspension of silt or finely divided organic matter.

U

URBAN RUNOFF - Storm water from city streets and gutters that usually contains a great deal of litter and organic and bacterial wastes.

V

VAPOR - The gaseous phase of substances that normally are either liquids or solids at atmospheric temperature and pressure; for example, steam and phenolic compounds.
VAPOR PLUME - The stack effluent consisting of flue gas made visible by condensed water droplets or mist.
VAPORIZATION - The change of a substance from the liquid to the gaseous state. One of three basic contributing factors to air pollution; the others are attrition and combustion.
VARIANCE - Sanction granted by a governing body for delay or exception in the application of a given law, ordinance, or regulation.
VECTOR - Disease vector - a carrier, usually an arthropod, that is capable of transmitting a pathogen from one organism to another.
VOLATILE - Evaporating readily at a relatively low temperature.

W

WASTE - Also see SOLID WASTE.
   (1) Bulky waste - items whose large size precludes or complicates their handling by normal collection, processing, or disposal methods.
   (2) Construction and demolition waste - building materials and rubble resulting from construction, remodeling, repair, and demolition operations.
   (3) Hazardous waste - wastes that require special handling to avoid illness or injury to persons or damage to property.
   (4) Special waste - those wastes that require extraordinary management.
   (5) Wood pulp waste - wood or paper fiber residue resulting from a manufacturing process.
   (6) Yard waste - plant clippings, prunings, and other discarded material from yards and gardens. Also known as yard rubbish.
WASTE WATER - Water carrying wastes from homes, businesses, and industries that is a mixture of water and dissolved or suspended solids.

WATER POLLUTION - The addition of sewage, industrial wastes, or other harmful or objectionable material to water in concentrations or in sufficient quantities to result in measurable degradation of water quality.

WATER QUALITY CRITERIA - The levels of pollutants that affect the suitability of water for a given use. Generally, water use classification includes: public water supply, recreation, propagation of fish and other aquatic life, agricultural use and industrial use.

WATER QUALITY STANDARD - A plan for water quality management containing four major elements: the use (recreation, drinking water, fish and wildlife propagation, industrial, or agricultural) to be made of the water; criteria to protect those uses; implementation plans (for needed industrial-municipal waste treatment improvements); and enforcement plans, and on anti-degration statement to protect existing high quality waters.

WATERSHED - The area drained by a given stream.

WATER SUPPLY SYSTEM - The system for the collection, treatment, storage, and distribution of potable water from the sources of supply to the consumer.

WATER TABLE - The upper level of ground water.

Z

ZOOPLANKTON - Planktonic animals that supply food for fish.

www.ingramcontent.com/pod-product-compliance
Lightning Source LLC
Chambersburg PA
CBHW082041300426
44117CB00015B/2566